BALANCING THE PRESIDENTIAL SEESAW

Case Studies in Community College Leadership

George B. Vaughan

for the Presidents Academy of the
American Association of Community Colleges

Community College Press®
a division of the American Association of Community Colleges
Washington, D.C.

The American Association of Community Colleges (AACC) is the primary advocacy organization for the nation's community colleges. The association represents 1,100 two-year, associate degree-granting institutions and some 10 million students. AACC provides leadership and service in five key areas: policy initiatives, advocacy, research, education services, and coordination/networking.

Requests for permission should be sent to
Community College Press
American Association of Community Colleges
One Dupont Circle, NW
Suite 410
Washington, DC 20036
Fax: (202) 223-9390

Printed in the United States of America.

ISBN 978-0-87117-317-1

CONTENTS

PREFACE

This work, commissioned by the Presidents Academy of the American Association of Community Colleges (AACC), presents a variety of case studies illustrating the types of sensitive situations in which community college presidents may find themselves and offers advice on how best to prepare for and resolve such situations. The cases, based on true accounts, are followed by some reactions from the presidents involved, and in some cases by the author's comments on whether and how the president could have handled the situation differently to bring about a more positive result.

In discussions with the Presidents Academy executive committee, members of the AACC board of directors, and presidents from across the nation, certain questions regarding the community college presidency emerged. Among the questions that this work deals with are the following:

1. What kinds of activities or practices do some presidents engage in that are guaranteed to get them into trouble? That is, what are the absolute *shall-nots* of presidential leadership?

2. Why do presidents find themselves in trouble even when they have played by the rules and have not engaged in any of the shall-nots?

3. When facing a difficult problem or issue, what constructive actions can presidents take to solve the problem or resolve the issue?

4. How can presidents analyze what mistakes, if any, they made in dealing with a given situation?

5. Since they occupy what is often a lonely position, where can presidents in trouble turn for advice and comfort?

6. What lessons have presidents learned from dealing with a specific problem or issue that might be of value to other presidents?

7. Finally, and most important, what can we learn from the answers to the above questions—especially the last one—and how can we use the information to assist other presidents who face similar problems or issues?

Addressing the Issues

To gather information for the study, a short questionnaire containing the above questions was sent to members of the Presidents Academy executive committee, to the members of the AACC board who are presidents, and to a small number of presidents who volunteered to submit issues for consideration. Their responses provided the basis for much of the information contained in this work. Regarding the 10 shall-nots, presidents attending the 1998 Presidents Academy Summer Experience were asked what they considered to be some activities presidents must not engage in under any circumstances. Much of what they had to say is included in the discussion of presidential shall-nots.

To strengthen the study further and to assist in producing the work, a six-member advisory committee was formed. Three of its members were appointed by the Presidents Academy executive committee: Stephen J. Maier, Jackson N. Sasser, and Carol Spencer. Two members were appointed by the AACC board: Wayne E. Giles and John J. Swalec. The sixth member of the committee—Charles R. Dassance—served on the academy's executive committee and is currently a member of the AACC board of directors, thus providing an important link between the academy and the board. The committee's advice and guidance were invaluable in the production of this work, and its members deserve the thanks of anyone who finds this volume useful or informative. All mistakes and questionable judgment calls, however, are mine alone.

Confidentiality

Some presidents were very open and even courageous in sharing information, for which I am grateful. Indeed, the short cases discussed in the volume are based on information received from presidents. I have taken every precaution to preserve the confidentiality of the colleges and individuals involved. To ensure confidentiality, the short cases contained in the study, though based on actual situations, have been disguised by using different locations, names, titles, and so on. In some cases, the gender and ethnic background of the president have been changed. In those cases where I felt the situation required it, to ensure that I did not violate the trust of the president, I sent the case to the president for his or her review to make certain that the requirement of confidentiality had been met. Occasionally, I have embellished the cases to place them in the perspective of the study, but none of the relevant facts have been changed. The mistakes made, actions taken, and advice offered are those of the presidents responding to the questionnaire. In those cases where I have added my own observations, I have identified them as Comments. Not all of the information received from presidents was included, but all of it was useful and helped shape this work.

The Audience

Although trustees and others interested in community colleges and their leaders can profit from reading this book, it was written primarily for future and current presidents. This book presents only the president's side of the story. No judgments were made as to whether the actions taken by a president were right or wrong. One can safely assume that in any given situation the perspective of the faculty or the governing board may differ from that of the president. Nevertheless, no attempt was made to present the other side of the story—or the rest of the story, even when it was known. Instead, the book presents each president's interpretation of what happened in a specific situation and what he or she did to correct the situation. The primary purpose of the work, then, is to answer the questions raised on pages iv and v and to offer advice and observations on the presidency based upon the observations and experiences of presidents. My comments are based on 17 years of experience as a community college president and on what I have written on the subject.

The Presidential Seesaw

While serving as president of a community college, I came up with an analogy to describe the college president's role. I envision the president as standing atop a seesaw, directly above the fulcrum, feet apart, always prepared to exert enough pressure to ensure that the seesaw moves at just the right speed, never touching the ground, never fluttering wildly, and never stopping. On one end of the seesaw are internal constituents: faculty, students, staff, and other members of the college community. On the other end are external constituents, including trustees, politicians, business leaders, and other community members. Both external and internal constituents can and do bring pressure to bear on the ends of the seesaw, causing it to be thrown out of balance unless the president takes action. The effective president keeps the seesaw in balance by gently applying just enough pressure to influence its movement.

Standing atop the presidential seesaw can be an exhilarating experience and can provide an excellent vantage point from which to oversee and influence the college's activities and direction. Nevertheless, it can also be a precarious position, especially for presidents who fail to understand the inherent risks associated with the presidency and who lack some understanding of how to prepare for the unexpected—those unforeseen activities and events that, if not dealt with adequately, can topple even the most stable of presidencies.

Rarely does a community college president serve in the position for more than a year or two without facing a situation that can turn into a major crisis if not dealt with quickly and effectively. This work examines some of the complications inherent in the position of the community college president. The cases illustrate difficult situations and show how presidents have extricated themselves from such dilemmas. Each case asks whom the president turned to for advice, what mistakes the president made, and what he or she learned. The final chapter includes suggestions for how the Presidents Academy can help improve the community college presidency in the future: for example, by creatively using those who have "been there"—retired presidents—as mentors and counselors for new presidents.

Most community college presidents exercise good judgment and conduct themselves appropriately. Yet even intelligent and committed people do things at times that can at best be classified as stupid. Although seemingly defying common sense and violating accepted rules of conduct, some presidents risk their careers for insignificant amounts of money, for a chance to display their authority or power, or for any number of other reasons. And even those who show excellent judgment are bound to find themselves embroiled in difficult situations from time to time, given the challenging and complex nature of the job. I hope this work will place in perspective the best choices a community college leader can make for responding to sensitive and politically charged situations.

Acknowledgments

A book of this nature requires the cooperation of numerous individuals and organizations. With this in mind, I would like to thank the executive committee of the Presidents Academy. I deeply appreciate the confidence in me shown by Carrole Wolin, and her support throughout the years. I am especially grateful to Steve Maier, Jack Sasser, and Carol Spencer for representing the academy on the advisory committee. I appreciate the support of the AACC board, and especially that of Wayne Giles and John Swalec, who served on the advisory committee. Charles Dassance, another member of the advisory committee, offered advice and encouragement to me throughout the project. David Pierce of the American Association of Community Colleges was supportive from the beginning to the completion of the project; his confidence in and support of my undertakings are always appreciated.

Presidents from across the nation submitted cases for this book. My thanks are extended to all those who responded to my call for help.

On the home front, I wish to thank Carmen Sasser, who has worked with me almost daily through the many revisions of the manuscript. Carmen is a fine copy editor and a joy to work with. Barbara Scott, associate editor of the *Community College Review*, provided invaluable assistance in organizing the material. Barbara is an outstanding colleague, a friend, and also a pleasure to work with. My thanks go also to Peggy Vaughan, for her review and her support, encouragement, and expertise.

THE 10 PRESIDENTIAL SHALL-NOTS

The activities described in the following list are sure ways for a president to lose his or her balance in the office; engaging in many of them may result in the president being forced either to resign from the presidency or to face being fired. These acts are so serious that, under most generally accepted standards of ethical conduct and reason, they must be seen as presidential commandments never to be broken. Although the list is intended to be specific to the presidency, it is obviously grounded in the ethics of daily life.

1. **The president shall not lie to or mislead the governing board, the faculty, other members of the college community, or the public.** Community college presidents should take seriously the motto of President Grover Cleveland's administration: Public office is a public trust. If the president is caught lying, the board may abruptly and unceremoniously remove him or her from office, because lying to or

misleading the board violates the bond of trust that is required for a successful trustee-president team. Once the bond is broken, it is often impossible to mend. If a president lies to or misleads the board, the word gets around campus and community, thus magnifying the impact of the deed. Similarly, to lie to or mislead the faculty or other members of the college community can be equally damaging. Although misleading or lying to members of the college community may not get a president fired immediately, it often results in a vote of no confidence in the president by the faculty. In any event, once members of the college community know that the president has lied to or misled them, the president's effectiveness at that institution is diminished to the point of no return. The president must also have the confidence of the public, for the community college president, more than any other college or university president, interacts almost daily with members of the local community. These community members must be able to depend upon the president for an accurate appraisal of the college's activities and accomplishments. Moreover, as the most visible symbol of the college in the community, the president embodies the values of the college. Lying to or misleading members of the public destroys the

As the most visible symbol of the college in the community, the president embodies the values of the college.

president's credibility and, to a degree, the credibility of the institution he or she represents. Business leaders and others who may form partnerships with institutional leaders need to feel that they can rely upon them to tell the truth, including all the relevant facts in any given situation. Betraying the trust of the office may ultimately be the unforgivable transgression for a community college president.

2. **The president shall not fail to keep the board informed about important issues facing the college or fail to involve trustees in resolving those issues.** Community college trustees are members of the community first and trustees second. As members of the college board, they are often the conduit through which information flows to the college president from the community and to the community from the

college. Trustees may accept an occasional slip-up on the president's part regarding the obligation to keep the board informed; however, if a president establishes a pattern of failing to inform the board about issues, he or she may, and probably should, be dismissed. The best surprise presidents can give trustees is no surprise, even when the news is good.

3. **The president shall not use the office of the president for self-aggrandizement, personal gain, or as a personal forum.** Most presidents view the presidency as a full-time position requiring all the time and energy they can muster, and they use all the resources at their disposal for fulfilling their role as president. Yet a few presidents engage in activities and practices not related to the presidency that take great amounts of their time and energy and result in conflicts of interest that jeopardize their effectiveness as presidents. Moreover, some make improper use of college resources for personal gain. Although it might be tempting to use the college truck for that Saturday morning chore or to authorize college personnel to work on the president's farm or private residence, doing so is illegal unless clearly authorized by the college governing board. Similarly, the president must not put pressure on college personnel to patronize a business or undertaking in which the president has an interest or from which he or she can profit financially or personally. President Theodore Roosevelt was fond of referring to the office of president of the United States as a bully pulpit, and this is also true of the office of the community college president. Nevertheless, presidents should not use the office as a forum for airing their personal problems unless their personal issues have a direct and potentially significant impact on the well-being of the institution.

4. **The president shall not ask for reimbursement of funds from any source if the request is not justified and legal in every respect.** Illegal reimbursements can run the gamut from requests for federal funds for student aid to padding one's travel expense account or even the college enrollment. Enrollment padding is especially tempting when budgets are tight. But no matter how tight the budget, the president should not

permit members of the college community to falsify enrollment reports. False reporting of enrollment constitutes obtaining funds under false pretenses—a clearly illegal act. A president who encourages others to report "phantom" course credits is misleading the college community, legislators, local political leaders, and the public regarding the college's success in enrolling students. (See the first shall-not, page 1.) Clearly, misappropriation of funds from any source violates college policies and state or federal laws. "Petty cash" is surely an appropriate description for the few dollars to be gained from cheating on one's expense account. It would be naive to believe that no one will ever find out or care about the "few extra dollars" added to one's travel expense account, and the consequences far outweigh the financial gain. When presidents misappropriate funds, no matter how seemingly insignificant the amount, either the auditors or someone else will inevitably find out about it, and the president may, and should, be fired.

5. **The president shall not engage in questionable relationships with any member of the college community.** Although occasionally unfettered romantic attachments may spring up between the president and a member of the college community, this situation must definitely be avoided if either the president or the other person is married. The president-secretary or president-assistant team can be especially vulnerable to temptation. Most presidents and secretaries spend more time together each working day than do most spouses or partners. For a president to pursue a member of the college community in such situations is to court disaster rather than romance. Wise presidents avoid trouble in this area, if for no other reason than that they do not want to put themselves or their potential collaborator in harm's way.

6. **The president shall not abuse alcohol or drugs in public or elsewhere.** For example, public drunkenness is simply unacceptable for a president. It damages the college's image and aids in the president's downfall. Alcohol abuse is an especially easy temptation to succumb to because alcohol is so readily available, often at no cost to the president.

In many situations, presidents not only are invited to consume alcohol but are expected to do so. New presidents, many of whom have never before experienced a lifestyle that involves a large number of receptions that include alcohol (it's there, it's free, there's a lot of it, and everyone seems to be consuming it), may be especially susceptible to the temptation to consume more alcohol than is acceptable.

7. **The president shall not employ friends, relatives, political nominees, acquaintances, or anyone else who is not fully qualified for a position and who has not gone through the college's procedures for employment.** The spouse of the president, no matter how well qualified, should never be employed by the college as a consultant or employee unless college policy clearly permits such employment. Similarly, use of the college to reward anyone through employment is a questionable and potentially illegal employment practice. Although the pressure to employ a friend or to make a political appointment is always present, the effective president resists the temptation and follows the college rules governing employment.

8. **The president shall not interfere with the teaching and learning process in ways that encroach upon the authority and responsibility of faculty members unless there is a clear and indisputable reason for doing so.** Anytime a president crosses the line and unduly interferes with the academic process, the offense is serious and demands retribution. One example concerns grade changes. *The Chronicle of Higher Education* (March 24, 1995) reported that the chancellor of a community college was reprimanded and forced to apologize after an investigation found that his son's grades had been changed from Fs to Cs in three mathematics courses. Although a report to the college governing board found no evidence that the chancellor had ordered the grade changes, it did find that the administrators and faculty members responsible for making the grade changes had done so because they feared retaliation from the chancellor. This case illustrates the danger of a president even appearing to be involved in altering grades. As *The*

Chronicle (A20) notes, the "scandal . . . deeply embarrassed" many at the college and "eroded an already strained relationship" between the faculty and the chancellor. The statewide faculty association criticized the college board, saying that if the trustees felt that the chancellor did coerce the mathematics department to change the grades, then he should have been fired. The involvement of the chancellor's son made this particular story newsworthy. But the lesson is the same, regardless of who the student is, and it applies to any kind of improper interference in the teaching and learning process.

9. **The president shall not become so arrogant or distant that the faculty is no longer involved in the decision-making process.** Although it may not always appear so, most faculty members want the same things most presidents want: an outstanding college devoted to serving students and committed to excellence. For themselves, faculty members, like presidents, want respect, good working conditions, and a degree of job security with adequate pay. Teaching and learning bind the president and faculty together. The president has a major obligation to ensure that the tie that binds is one that does not chafe the faculty to the point of irritation nor bind them so tightly that they do not feel free to question decisions that affect the college's or their own well-being. The president must recognize that faculty members not only have a right to raise questions regarding the governing of the college, but also have an obligation to do so.

> *The president must recognize that faculty members not only have a right to raise questions regarding the governing of the college, but also have an obligation to do so.*

10. **The president shall not stay in a position so long that all the excitement and challenges are gone.** How long is too long to stay in a given presidency? This question haunts most sensitive presidents who have been in a position for seven years or so, although many presidents are highly effective long after they begin the self-questioning. Yet even

when the individual president and others feel that he or she has been in a position too long, the president may refuse to relinquish the office and may stay in the position far too long. A result is that the president (and often the college) settles into a mode of operation that requires little or no leadership on the president's part. When the president stays beyond the point where presidential leadership diminishes or disappears, the board has an obligation to release the president and seek new leadership.

Most community college presidents do not willfully break any of the 10 shall-nots, and some are occasionally victims of hostile trustees or a faculty whose goal is to see the president fired. Some presidents do, however, endanger their careers and reputations by engaging in one or more of the presidential shall-nots. Even then, those presidents who do stray from accepted practices rarely set out to violate accepted rules of conduct and reason. Rather, they often slip gradually into the traps that await them.

Why do presidents let themselves slip into undesirable situations? Many become too comfortable in their positions; some become too greedy; others feel powerful and begin to believe that rules and regulations apply only to others; some become overconfident and feel they are invincible. Some presidents simply become lazy in how they approach their position, while others are lulled into believing that they are immune to the consequences resulting from playing too lose with the rules and regulations or from failing to exercise good judgment. The price of unethical behavior can be heavy, often resulting in the president being fired or at least being asked to leave the presidency. A few presidents clearly "ask for it" and should be forced to leave their position for violating accepted standards of ethical conduct, but they are the exception.

Most presidents at some point find themselves in difficult situations for reasons other than breaking the rules. The following chapters examine some of the situations that presidents face that are not so clear-cut as to require extreme action on the part of the board, faculty, or president. Still, they are serious and can cause presidents to experience many sleepless nights and long, lonely days.

2

THE DEFINING MOMENT

A defining moment can occur at any point in a president's career and thus is difficult to predict or avoid. The case presented here shows how someone's hidden agenda can threaten a president's position. The president in this case offers insightful comments on the nature of a defining moment in the life of a president:

> Looking back on nearly two decades as a community college president, [I see that] many of the incidents that seemed earth-shattering at the time tend to fade in favor of happier times. Age and tender mercy perhaps can be cited as reasons that positive events overshadow negative ones, even though the latter usually present moments, sometimes weeks and months, of heart- and headache. Defining moments, however, do not fade as readily as lesser incidents. A person has a tendency to be wide awake when a defining moment occurs, the outcome of which could mean the end of one's current position or even one's career. Sometimes a defining moment takes a matter of days. At other times, a defining moment can be exactly that—a moment.

THE TRUSTEE AS MOLE

Circumstances

The president of a community college decided she needed a change of scenery. She had just completed her sixth year in her current position, her second presidency. Both of her presidencies had been in small colleges, the first located in a rural area and the current one in the suburbs of a midsize city. She was ready for something bigger. She also wanted to return to the area where she had grown up. Glancing at *The Chronicle of Higher Education,* she noticed that her "Camelot college"—the place one dreams of—in the Pacific Northwest had a presidential vacancy. She decided to apply for the position.

She knew some things about the college before applying. For example, she knew that the founding president, who was just completing his 26th year in office, was retiring. Although they had never been close friends, they had talked briefly at professional meetings and on other occasions. She was surprised but pleased when the retiring president informed her that she had his full support for the position. As it turned out, his support was crucial. "As the search process proceeded, she recounts, I received frequent calls from him informing me of committee and board activity. I was grateful for the insider's flow of information. Each time a negative arose, he rode to my rescue and was able to successfully promote my candidacy." She believes that she was selected to be the next president of the college in part due to his support.

The president accepted the position without hesitation; after all, it was a larger college than she had ever led and it was located just where she wanted to be. However, she soon discovered that the previous president expected to be paid for his support.

The Defining Moment

The retiring president was honored by the college, which appointed him president emeritus and named a playing field for him. The honors were justified, the new president believes, for the retiring president had been an outstanding leader in many ways. She was ready and willing to do her part in honoring him. "I felt the least I could do was agree to his suggestion that it would be invaluable if the college were to provide him with an office, a typewriter, and a telephone so he could complete the long-delayed historical information on the college. It would be only for a year and involve a relatively small monthly stipend. Looking back, I now realize that I should have been able to see the tornado coming."

Along with a beautiful office and a breathtaking view of the Pacific coastline, the new president inherited an administrative assistant who had worked with the former president for two decades. The administrative assistant's office was across the hall from the president's office. As he had done in the past, the assistant used the services of the president's secretary as if she were assigned to him rather than to the president's office. The new president, being bright and alert, "didn't take long to realize that much of my assistant's time was being devoted to frequent phone calls with the president emeritus."

The situation deteriorated rapidly: College board members, as well as members of the public, began to ask questions about minor decisions she was making. Obviously the assistant was keeping the former president fully informed, and he in turn was talking with members of the college board and people in the community. The president notes that "it was becoming abundantly obvious that the former president and I were in the midst of a serious 'failure to communicate.'" She came to "realize that his support in my getting the job was meant to equate into constant consultation and reliance on him for all decisions, big and small. The moment I failed to seek his opinion, I became fair game for criticism. Each day brought an escalation of criticism and questions from board members and persons in the community."

After about four months on the job, the president learned that a respected community leader who was the former president's close friend was running for a vacancy on the college governing board. He won the seat by a large margin. At his very first board meeting, the new board member read "statements of concern" that the president believes "were obviously written by someone else." The questioning—much of which concerned the college finances—continued in subsequent board meetings. The president recalls that "it became obvious that how I handled these public confrontations would determine whether I needed to start looking for another job or whether I would be able to take the college into the 21st century." How to deal with the actions of the new board member became, for this president, a *defining moment.*

Seeking Help

This president, filled with doubt about members of her staff and preparing to indirectly challenge a revered former president and directly challenge a board member, had no one to turn to. Instead, she turned inward for strength. She "soon realized that the best way to defend myself was to work hard, make the best decisions for the college and students I could, and provide, without anger, every piece of information demanded by the new board member. For six months, most of my time and the time of several of our staff was consumed with preparing financial reports of one kind or another [for the new board member]." However, she did find an important confidant and supporter in the board chair, especially as the situation progressed.

Taking Action

The first action the president took was to include in the reports prepared for the new board member information regarding earlier financial reports, from before she had joined the college. This information demonstrated both that the college was moving forward and that the past had not really been all that great. Next, the president decided it was "time to have a private conversation" with the new trustee. She notes that he "was never discourteous nor did he appear to have a personal vendetta. He was simply acting out of friendship to the former president and upon information being supplied to the former president." Her third action was to tell the trustee directly that "it was time for the game to end."

Regrets

Although the president in this case did not list any mistakes she felt she had made, she may have erred in relying too heavily upon the assistance of the former president in getting the position, thereby placing herself in his debt, at least from his perspective. This judgment call resulted in her granting the former president an office on campus and thus access to the president's assistant and others. Working in an office on campus, obtaining information from the assistant, and orchestrating the actions of the new trustee, the former president was well placed to convince members of the board and community leaders that he continued to exercise influence on campus. Denying him an office would have lessened his influence by shutting off some of his avenues for obtaining information. This office apparently gave him legitimacy in the eyes of many.

Lessons

The most important lesson the president learned from her defining moment was that it is always better to confront a board member and try to clear the air than to let him or her undermine the president. When she met with the trustee, he "responded by telling me that he thought I was doing a wonderful job and that he appreciated all of the information we had provided him." He agreed that any future requests for information would come before the entire board. In the final analysis, the president learned that the new trustee had nothing against her personally.

She also found that her previous experience as a president was an invaluable resource. She notes that "the more experience you have in dealing with difficult situations, the more success you'll have in handling the worst of them. I'm not sure I would have successfully coped with this scenario during my first few years as a president." She also learned to keep her personal feelings in perspective: "You must make yourself realize that if you were not president of the college, this would not be happening. One of the most difficult lessons any president must learn as early as possible is that 'it ain't you, it's the position.'"

> In the overall scheme of things, the crisis isn't as severe as you think. Look outside. Are birds still singing? Is the sun still shining? Seeing the big picture allows you to gain the perspective that although bad things may be happening, there are many other positive things occurring. The needs of the faculty, staff,

students, and community still exist. Ask yourself what's going on here? Much of the time, it's probably simpler than we think.

Many times, just being able to blow off a bit of private steam can help a great deal. In this situation, the board chair was understanding and supportive. In fact, being able to discuss the ins and outs of each major problem was the key to an eventual positive outcome.

Advice

- Remember that experience counts, so draw upon it every chance you get.

- Do not let yourself be intimidated.

- Do not take issues personally.

- Force yourself to take a broader view of any situation.

- Have a knowledgeable person with whom you can discuss various situations, but pick that person carefully and be judicious about what you confide.

- Do not recruit allies for your side of the argument.

- Leave your problems at the office. It is important to your health and that of your family or loved ones.

- Work hard every day and do the best you can. Do not allow any situation to so consume you that you are unable to function in your job.

Comments

This president respected several of the shall-nots: She did not withhold information from a board member, even an apparently hostile one, and she did not let a personal need overwhelm her ability to maintain a professional perspective on the situation. Instead she continued to build public trust, despite the circumstances, by doing her job in a straightforward and conscientious way. In so doing, she kept the public's trust, and she gave the former president no grounds for continuing to criticize her performance.

3

TRANSITIONS

Often the most difficult task facing a new president is how to lead the college through the inevitable transition period following his or her arrival. The culture of a college has developed over many years; changes made by new presidents may challenge some elements of that culture. Moreover, the transition may be extremely difficult if the previous president held the position for a long time and was well respected by members of the college community, the board, and the local community. Difficult transitions can also occur with the hiring of other executives, such as a new vice president. The following cases illustrate some of the problems that can arise during a transition.

SHARED GOVERNANCE

Circumstances

A new president took on the formidable task of changing the governing process at the college. Her predecessor had been president for 22 years;

before that, he had been a faculty member and administrator at the college. The new president quickly reached a conclusion shared by many members of the college community: The previous president was autocratic, involving few people in the college decision-making process. He did not hesitate to "bully and intimidate faculty and staff who disagreed with him," she explains. Moreover, he was a "good ol' boy" with strong ties in the community.

The new president felt changes were needed. She believed strongly that, in her words, "shared governance is a more inclusive way of involving people in the college." She opened up channels of communication, supporting faculty union membership on committees and letting it be known that she respected the union's role in college governance. The results of her actions were unexpected and out of line with what she had hoped for when she decided that more people should be involved in governing the college.

The president found that the faculty and staff soon began to push the envelope in exercising their new freedom. The faculty union became especially troubling; it now wanted to be involved in shaping the budget, deciding how funds were expended—including those allocated for trustee travel—and deciding the number of administrative positions. The president now faced the challenge of keeping balance in the governing process without closing off faculty participation.

Seeking Help

The president first turned to books and journal articles related to college governance. At the same time, she worked very closely with the board of trustees, carefully noting that this particular problem had the potential to affect the board for years to come. She also turned to other presidents for advice, including those who had served as her mentors. She sought help in prayer, finding that spiritual wisdom provided guidance and helped her keep a healthy perspective on the problems associated with academic governance. Finally—as she noted in a candid self-assessment, expressing frustration that most presidents experience at one time or another—she sat down and "just cried."

Taking Action

Although she gained courage and support from her advisers and practices, the president knew she had to act to solve the problems associated with the new climate on campus. She took several steps to resolve the problem or at least to place it in perspective in relation to the operation of the college. She asked each college committee to develop a clear statement of its responsibilities, and she let each committee know what she expected from it and what the committee could expect from her. She worked with her cabinet to identify documents, college policies and procedures, state regulations, and any other statements dealing with the governance of the college.

The board held a retreat to discuss governance. At the retreat board members discussed their understanding of the term and how governance at the college was carried out, under both the previous and the current administrations. They also discussed what they expected of the president in the governing process.

The president set up meetings with the leadership of each group on campus to discuss governance at the college. She clarified what she meant by shared governance, and also set a process in motion to ensure that each segment of the college community understood the meaning of the term and what its limits were at their institution. She brought the board into the debate, thus demonstrating to the college community that she was not alone in attempting to widen participation in the governing process. This step also conveyed that she wanted that involvement to be meaningful, but without giving away the store.

Regrets

The culture of a college is fragile, yet it changes very gradually. In this case, the shift from an autocratic governing process to one of shared governance challenged the existing culture.

> *"The biggest mistake I made was that I believed them when they told me they wanted change from the old leadership."*

The president notes that "the biggest mistake I made was that I believed them when they told me they wanted change from the old leadership. The transition of change has been very difficult for the old guard faculty. Over half of the full-time faculty have been here 15 to 25 years." She also feels that she should have stood up to the faculty earlier. "There were times when I was too generous and patient, and tried to be too understanding of their points of view."

Lessons

This president noted that she is still learning from her experiences in moving the college from an autocratic administration to one that is more open. In the process, she has found that faculty and staff can be fickle. "One day they love you, the next day they don't. They have short memories on the good things you do for them and long memories on things you disagree on." She believes it is important for presidents to make the "right decisions for the right reasons" and not to let pressure groups force them into making wrong decisions. But no matter how effective the leader or how noble the cause, there are always some groups or individuals at the college who oppose the president.

Advice

- Establish a strong network of presidents to whom you can turn for advice.
- Work with the board chair when a difficult issue or problem arises, for no president can solve problems and resolve issues alone.
- Approach change with caution, since changes must be made within the context of the institutional culture.

Comments

This president paid particular attention to the first shall-not. She made it a priority to understand the college culture and to build trust among her colleagues. She also recognized the importance of getting to know the faculty as colleagues and not making any assumptions about how they would react to a change in leadership style. Most of all, this president learned that it is essential to define one's terms and to draw some boundaries before setting out to change the culture of a college. Anytime a president sets out to make major changes at an institution, he or she should understand how the changes will affect the culture of the college. New presidents should do all they can to familiarize themselves with the existing culture of the college.

DELEGATING AUTHORITY

Circumstances

The president in this case had been for the past three years at the helm of a college located in the affluent suburbs of a large city. He prided himself on working well with all segments of the college community, especially the faculty. He was so comfortable in his relations with the faculty that when a new executive vice president was hired, the president, in his words, "turned the running of the college over to him." The new vice president succeeded a well-liked vice president who had been with the college for 12 years before his retirement. The president explains that "in an effort to provide the new vice president with support and freedom to implement his ideas, I carefully stepped back from faculty life. I focused on resource development, leaving too much responsibility in the hands of someone with limited experience. I let distance grow between the faculty and me. The consequences were many."

Not surprisingly, the faculty became frustrated with what they saw as a lack of support from, and lack of contact with, the president. A communications vacuum occurred, which was quickly filled with rumors and false information. The president felt himself losing the support and trust of the faculty, which he had spent the last three years building up.

Seeking Help

In the president's words, "my greatest source of advice has always been other presidents who help me see the various dimensions of a situation and offer possible solutions." In this case as well, the president turned to his presidential colleagues for advice.

Taking Action

The president sensed the frustrations of the faculty, and he acted at once. First, he set out to rebuild relations. This included ensuring that the administrative leadership team of the college was responsive to faculty concerns and that faculty members were once again included in the decision-making process. Second, he staged forums on matters of interest to the faculty. Third, the president made it a point to attend as many faculty events as possible. As he aptly observes, "Faculty can endure flat budgets, difficult decisions, and challenging circumstances, provided they are informed and given an opportunity to participate in determining the college's response to situations." His actions likely headed off major problems in the future.

Regrets

Looking back, the president feels that the transition period involving the new vice president was not well handled. "I should have taken more time in facilitating the change in leadership. I moved too quickly." But his biggest mistake, he feels, was "concentrating too much on external affairs and not making campus communications my first priority."

Lessons

The main lesson this president learned was one of balance between external and internal constituencies: Although the Chamber of Commerce and potential donors may be important to the success of a presidency, they are not as important as the college faculty.

Advice

- Do not assume that things are going well just because you do not hear complaints.
- Do not assume that external activities, no matter how productive, excuse you from your internal obligations.
- Always listen to those with whom you work, and communicate with them in every way possible.

Comments

With all good intentions, this president briefly violated a shall-not: He became too distant from the faculty. He quickly and emphatically corrected the problem, once he realized that a well-intentioned management decision had created the dangerous impression that he did not value close involvement with faculty. This brief case also illustrates the need for presidents to be sensitive to what faculty members are thinking, even if they are not vocal in expressing their frustrations.

4

Too Close for Comfort

One of the president's most important tasks is to cultivate relationships with the members of the governing board. Yet nothing frustrates presidents more than having a trustee get too close for comfort to the day-to-day operations of the college. As one president notes, "there are a number of generic issues that are common to many governing boards and about which there is frequent discussion among presidents. Probably the most common, in this regard, is perceived board interference in the administrative operation of the college. Interference can come through questioning minute details, talking with individual employees about problems at the college, and the like." Adding to the difficulty is the vagueness of the line separating a trustee's role from that of the president. This can cause frustrations for both trustees and presidents. Each president must decide for him- or herself—at least up to a point—when a trustee has crossed into the president's territory. The following cases deal with situations in which trustees clearly crossed the line that separated their role in making policy and overseeing the college from the president's role of administering the college.

TIME ON HER HANDS

Circumstances

A very successful and powerful minority business leader retired at the age of 56, when her company merged with another one. As a successful business leader she had served as chair of the college foundation. Energetic, intelligent, and willing to serve, after her retirement she ran for and was elected to the college governing board. At this college, trustees were permitted (indeed encouraged) to serve on the foundation board as well.

A problem arose when the newly elected trustee informed the president that she had time on her hands and wanted to do even more for the college than she was currently doing. She confessed that she was having a difficult time "winding down" after leaving the business world. She suggested a solution: to put more time and energy into her work as chair of the foundation board. To be successful, she felt it would be necessary to have an office on campus and to have secretarial help provided. This arrangement, she noted, would permit her to work daily with both the director of the foundation and the president.

As one would expect, the president was not overjoyed with the notion of a trustee having an office on campus where she could visit with the president daily. But at the same time, the president did not want to make an enemy of a powerful trustee, especially one who had served the college well in her work with the foundation.

Seeking Help

The president discussed the situation with the board chair and director of the foundation, both of whom strongly opposed the idea of the trustee taking up residency on campus. The president wondered openly what action she might take that would allow her to work with the board member without giving up too much. Neither the chair nor the director offered a solution.

Taking Action

The president believed that at this point the best action was no action. She did not offer the new trustee an on-campus office and simply let the matter drop. There it remained.

Lessons

This president feels that she did not make any mistakes in her handling of the problem. But she learned that trustees who are powerful, energetic, successful, and highly intelligent can be a mixed blessing to a college president.

Advice

- Maintain your integrity as president at all times and in all circumstances, even if it means saying no to a powerful trustee.
- Keep things in perspective—for example, by engaging in prayer or meditation.
- Recognize that things will not go smoothly at all times, regardless of how effective a president is.
- Keep up your spirits, and avoid prolonged periods of discouragement. One way to do this is to define the role of president and not let the position define you.

Comments

It is crucial for presidents to recognize, as the president did in this case, that there really are times when the best action is no action at all.

CROSSING THE LINE

The president of one community college recalls vividly a situation he faced almost 15 years ago. In the fifth year of his presidency he had to confront a trustee who had crossed the line that separates the board's role from that of the president.

Circumstances

A prominent dentist ran for and was elected to the college governing board, with the endorsement and backing of the faculty union. The new trustee, disregarding much of the advice he received in the college's formal orientation for new trustees, immediately went directly to faculty members to discuss issues that the faculty saw as important to the college. The trustee did not consult the president before meeting with the faculty, nor did he inform the president of what took place in the meetings. In doing so, the trustee clearly violated college practice, according to which trustees would contact the president before meeting with faculty members to discuss college policy.

The president soon learned that the trustee was bypassing him and talking directly with the faculty about issues affecting the college. He immedi-

The president soon learned that the trustee was bypassing him and talking directly with the faculty about issues affecting the college.

ately contacted the trustee, informing him that this was not the way such matters were handled at the college. He requested that the trustee contact him instead, saying, "Contact me and I will see that you get the information you want." The trustee retorted that he did not need anyone's permission to talk with members of the faculty.

The president had to agree with the trustee, for despite the college practice, there was no college policy requiring trustees to contact the president before talking with faculty members about college issues and problems. Nevertheless, the president explained to the new trustee how much time and energy it took for college staff to get all of the information the trustee requested as a result of talking with faculty members about issues facing the college. Once again, he asked that official communications between trustees and faculty should be routed through the president's office. He asked the trustee, "How can I manage the college and my staff if you are unwilling to abide by our accepted way of doing things? Please back off a bit and let's work through channels." In spite of the president's advice, the trustee refused to "back off."

The president decided that he had done all he could to prevent what might become a major crisis for the board and for his office. He contacted the board chair and explained what was taking place. The board chair agreed with the president's stance: Trustees should not bypass the president when communicating with the faculty regarding college policy or issues affecting the college. The board chair asked the trustee to take the president's advice and work through established channels. This had an immediate impact; the trustee did indeed back off—at least temporarily.

Not long afterward, the same trustee demanded a place on the administrative board team constituted to negotiate a new contract with the faculty union. This practice of board participation in negotiations was not unusual at this college. Indeed, such teams always included trustees.

Within days the trustee once again crossed over the line of accepted practice. As the president explains, "In spite of the prior agreement that we act as a team and speak with one voice, in a session with the union team (which included one of the trustee's most ardent union supporters) and without consultation, the trustee said the board would accept a union proposal. This move was in violation of our understanding that unless we agreed in caucus, no board negotiating team member or administrative staff member was to take license to agree or disagree with any proposal." The trustee had clearly violated the understanding that the president and board had agreed to. Both the president and the board chair viewed this as unacceptable.

Seeking Help

In both the issues involving this board member, the president turned to the board chair for help. In the first instance, the board chair's intervention seemed to solve the problem. In the second instance, however, the president had to take direct action.

Taking Action

The president immediately brought the administrative-board negotiating team together and informed them of his belief that the trustee, by acting alone, was in conflict with the board's position. The president suggested that the negotiations be stopped immediately. The trustee disagreed with the president's statement that the trustee had crossed the line, but he agreed to put the negotiations on hold. Next, the president informed the trustee that he would communicate the situation—including the disagreement between the president and the trustee—to the full board at its meeting the next evening. The board supported the president's position by a vote of seven to one. The next day the president informed the union leaders that the board was retracting the offer made by the lone trustee.

Regrets

Things worked out well for this president. He admits, however, that if he had it to do over, he would encourage the board to take a more active role in resolving the situation. The president notes that it might be "unhealthy" for other presidents to take the stance and actions he took—especially not contacting the board chair as soon as the problem with the trustee arose.

Lessons

This president learned that board members, if left to run free, will occasionally drift over the line. For example, this president, like many others, has occasionally been asked to give preferential treatment to friends or relatives of board members. He has found that even the board chair (this president has had four in his career) may become "assertive" on occasion, making demands that are in conflict with the best interests of the college.

Advice

- Be honest with board members at all times, letting them know what your stand is and why you have taken a particular stand. When operating in an atmosphere of mutual respect, trustees and presidents can work out their differences without hostility and conflict.

- Ask the board if it is a good idea to have trustees involved in collective bargaining. They may be willing to serve as observers instead, and leave the negotiations to professionals.

- Work to ensure that the board understands that the president is responsible for the operation of the college on a daily basis and that trustees should not interfere with the daily operations.

Comments

This president avoided violating the second shall-not. He made information available to the new trustee about the way he and the board customarily worked, and he then informed first the board chair and then the full board about the trustee's actions when he realized that those actions were jeopardizing the college's welfare.

THE DISSIDENT TRUSTEE

Circumstances

At a college in the East, during a campus protest led by a small group of faculty and staff, a board member decided that he would handle the situation his way. "His way" was to call faculty and staff members and invite them to his home to discuss any concerns they had. In spite of being warned that he might be personally liable for any actions the faculty and staff might take, the board member persisted. Indeed, when a representative of the dissatisfied campus groups appeared before the full board, she quoted conversations that had taken place with the trustee. Other members of the board warned the dissident trustee that his actions conflicted with board policy and practice.

Eventually the trustee decided it was time to "rejoin" the board; he did so, and he ceased having private conversations with the protesters. Thereupon the protesters turned against the trustee and began harassing him at home. In this case, what had begun as a faculty issue quickly became a board issue. The president had to deal with the dissident trustee before dealing with the campus problem.

Seeking Help

This president turned to the board chair for help with this difficult issue.

29

Taking Action

After discussion with the board chair, the president placed the issue of the dissident trustee in the hands of the board chair, who in turn asked other members of the board to help with the situation. The board moved quickly to solve the problem.

Regrets

The president does not feel that he made any mistakes in handling this issue. He involved the board chair early on, and the board took action to solve the problem.

Lessons

This president learned that trustees, no matter how well meaning, can cause major problems for the college if they bypass accepted board policies and practices. The board, he now recognizes, must act as a unit.

Advice

- Educate the members of the board to ensure that they understand their roles fully.

- Bring in an outside consultant to provide training for the board. An outsider can lead the board in directions that a president cannot, without appearing self-serving.

- Recognize that the president and board must work as a team. Board members who bypass the president in dealing with the faculty and staff beg for trouble, both for themselves and for the college president.

- Ensure that all trustees understand that authority lies with the entire board and not with a single trustee.

CONFLICT OF INTEREST

Circumstances

The chancellor of a multicollege district found herself faced with a problem when one of the college's trustees proposed what the president saw as a conflict of interest. One of the district's campuses is located in a center built with federal funds and owned by the city. The community college district leased the building from the city for one dollar a year, with the understanding that the college would maintain the building at a cost of over $300,000 a year. One of the oldest programs offered on the campus was for training workers for the garment trade. When much of the garment work moved to industries in the Sun Belt, there was no longer a need for the space; indeed, the space had not been used for two years. A board member, who was close friends with an individual in the import business, knew about the facility and the agreement with the city. The importer asked for a meeting with the chancellor, which was arranged. After noting how highly his friend on the board spoke of the chancellor and the good work the college was doing, the importer proposed to the chancellor that he be allowed to use the building as a distribution center for his import business. The chancellor asked him to put his proposal in writing.

Meanwhile, the chancellor decided to investigate the situation more thoroughly. Upon visiting the facility, she found that the importer's trustee friend had been visiting the facility almost daily, spending several hours there on each visit. To add insult to injury, the trustee was a chain smoker and ignored all of the no smoking signs in the building. The faculty, who were not allowed to smoke in the building and many of whom resented the second-hand smoke emanating from the trustee's constant smoking, were quite upset. The situation was rapidly deteriorating to the point where the chancellor not only had a trustee problem but a faculty problem as well.

Seeking Help

The chancellor had separate lunches with the chair and vice chair of the board and asked for their help in solving the situation.

Taking Action

The first action the chancellor took was to gather all the information she could on the situation. She then turned the information over to the board chair. In order not to appear to be a snitch, the chancellor in a private conversation mentioned the smoking episodes to the trustee, who was very apologetic and immediately ceased smoking on his daily visits.

Regrets

Things worked out just fine; thus the chancellor did not feel that she made any mistakes.

Lessons

Board members may be reticent to police themselves unless forced to do so. Be patient. In this case, the chancellor got lucky: the businessman's import business soon went belly up, thus solving the problem.

Advice

- When a trustee is involved in questionable activities, bring the situation to the attention of the board chair immediately.
- Remind all members of the board that they must monitor each other's activities.
- Remind members of the board how actions by individual trustees or the president reflect on other trustees and the college.
- Keep in mind that many problems and issues are multidimensional, often involving trustees, faculty, and community members.

Comments

This president showed discretion regarding the fourth shall-not. Although she made the board chair aware of the trustee's questionable alliance with the importer, she did not reveal that the trustee's smoking was a problem. Instead, she approached the trustee about that behavior directly because it involved a personal habit and not a behavior that might put the college in a questionable position.

THE NEW TRUSTEE

Circumstances

A new board member was determined to impress his colleagues on the board by illustrating just how valuable he would be to the college. At his very first board meeting, the new trustee began making motions on items that were not even on the agenda. This practice continued for the next two board meetings. The president did not want a major shakeup on the board, so she decided to talk with the new trustee.

Seeking Help

When asked to whom she turned for help, the president replied, "No one. I figured this one out all by myself!"

Taking Action

As suggested above, the first action the president took was to talk with the new trustee. She suggested that the trustee study the issue carefully and then come back with a recommendation at the next meeting, thus avoiding embarrassing himself and other trustees. The president realized that this was an intermediate step; a permanent solution had to be found. She knew that the new trustee was bright and wanted to contribute to the well-being of the college. The permanent solution was to place the trustee on a major committee and use his knowledge and expertise where it would do the most good. The trustee became an excellent committee member; he relaxed, took his time in studying issues, and became familiar with the governing structure of the college. He became an outstanding board member, saving the college thousands of dollars on one project alone.

Regrets

As the president stated above, she figured this one out all by herself and did not make any mistakes along the way.

Lessons

Look beneath the obvious. Try to figure out why an individual acts in a certain way. In this case, the new trustee simply wanted to be needed and to do good work for the college. Nevertheless, he needed guidance in the best way to accomplish his goals. The president gracefully let the new trustee know that the board's tasks would be impossible to carry out successfully if all its members were not united in what they want to see the college accomplish. If the board and president cannot work as a team, moving the college in an agreed-upon direction, then the president should either resign or be replaced by the board unless the problem lies with the board. If the problem is with the board, the president must rely on the board chair, assuming the chair is not the problem, and other board members to solve the problem. The college should not be made to suffer as a result of board-president conflicts. This president recalls that "In this case the new trustee did not distrust me (although at first it appeared that way); he just wanted to be useful with his time and feel that he was contributing to the college's well-being."

Advice

- Remind members of the board that the president is responsible for carrying out the policies, procedures, and wishes of the board.

- Encourage trustees to work through the president and support the president as needed.

- Look for possible reasons for unusual behavior.

- Do everything you can to ensure that trustees understand the mission of the college and their role in achieving that mission. Ask for and use their talents so they develop a comfort and confidence level in you as president.

Comments

This case illustrates another aspect of the shall-not concerning keeping one's emotional agenda out of the picture. In this case, the president stepped back from the situation enough to gain some perspective on the new trustee's motivations. When she realized that the motivations were good ones, she provided the trustee with opportunities to redirect his energies. Had she become irritated or emotionally embroiled in the situation, her response may have been less successful. Certainly she would have found the presidency more frustrating and less gratifying.

5

$\Delta\Delta$

POLITICS AS USUAL

Politics is a perennial aspect of a community college presidency. Major initiatives usually involve both internal and external politics, and it is generally up to the president to guide the college through the political process in order to achieve goals.

BREAKING NEW GROUND

Circumstances

A suburban community college district in a midwestern state had recently added a new suburban college to its system. Just days after the college opened, the suburban police chiefs in the college's district approached the college president. The chiefs wanted the college to establish a police academy that would serve the needs of suburban police departments. The chiefs noted that the city served by the college had its own academy but did not permit anyone outside the city limits to enroll. The chiefs pointed out that recent legislation required that police officers engage in an annual continuing education program. They also noted that the demand for police officers far exceeded the supply.

To get the academy under way, the police chiefs agreed to certain conditions. The departments would hire recruits, send them to the college's academy, and pay their salaries during the training period. In turn, the cadets would pay their own costs to attend college. The cost in this state was approximately $3,600 per academic year. The police chiefs also agreed to the college's requirement that the academy be located in a rented facility that had formerly been a two-story elementary school.

State approval was obtained for creating the academy, an advisory committee was formed, and the academy was off and running. After one year of operation it was an overwhelming success, praised by the police chiefs, the college board and administration, and the curriculum advisory committee. The advisory committee had only one major complaint: The current facility was no longer acceptable. The committee proposed (politely demanded) that the college build a new training facility, to be located on campus next to a recently completed science building. The committee members noted that many of the cadets would receive an associate degree and hence would want to be, and should be, involved in the college scene. A campus location would also give the students easy access to the general education courses they needed.

The campus straddled two legislative districts; the chair of the House Budget Committee, a Democrat, represented one district, and the other district was represented by the House minority leader, who was a Republican. The chancellor, recognizing the potentially explosive nature of the situation, demanded that the campus president and the advisory committee establish beyond a reasonable doubt the need for the new building.

The chancellor, recognizing the potentially explosive nature of the situation, demanded that the campus president and the advisory committee establish beyond a reasonable doubt the need for the new building.

The advisory committee called a meeting and invited the two legislative leaders to attend. Both came to the meeting and left impressed with the work of the college's academy. They agreed to seek funds for a feasibility study to determine the need for a new building. They were true to their word, and under their leadership the state legislature appropriated $50,000 in planning money.

The feasibility study was completed. The need for a new facility for police training was clearly established. In addition to serving as a police academy, the new building would meet other needs, providing facilities for emergency medical training (EMT) and firefighter training.

To build the new facility would require $12.4 million; following established policy, half was to come from the state and half from the localities. The two legislators agreed to obtain the state's share. Things were going along smoothly, or so the chancellor thought.

As the project moved through the legislature, opposition emerged, in spite of strong bipartisan support from the two legislators from the college's district. Not all legislators were eager to appropriate $6.2 million for the project, even though two of their leaders were in favor of it. A regional state university, located some 50 miles away, opposed the project on the grounds that the police academy would compete with its own program in police training. The firefighters' union opposed the project for fear that it would eliminate three other small firefighter training programs, resulting in a loss of 30 jobs. Finally, a group of faculty opposed any medical training at the new college on the grounds that it would compete with existing programs at the downtown campus. The chancellor now faced the challenge of navigating these turbulent political waters successfully.

Seeking Help

The chancellor consulted the members of the college governing board who represented the part of the district in which the new facility was to be located and asked for their help. He also consulted regularly with the two legislators, as well as other legislative leaders. He sought, and followed, advice from the college lobbyist. The chancellor's management team, especially the campus presidents, offered advice and assistance as needed.

Taking Action

The college's veteran lobbyist, armed with copies of the feasibility study, met with all legislators who opposed the project. The lobbyist also informed the legislators that the police departments strongly supported the project. The police chiefs solicited the support of their legislators. The college invited the state university to send representatives to the campus to see for themselves how the new building would be used. As a result, an agreement was reached whereby the state university would offer upper-division courses on the community college campus leading to a bachelor's degree. The university president reluctantly gave his support. The faculty problem was solved, in part, by involving faculty from the downtown campus to help plan the space for EMT in the new building. In addition, the chancellor instructed the two campus presidents to cooperate. The chancellor wisely advised the firefighters' union to separate the loss of jobs from the need for training. Although this action did not gain union support for the project, it prevented the chancellor from becoming involved in someone else's fight.

Regrets

The chancellor feels that better communications would have made the process flow more smoothly. "Although one often thinks he is communicating effectively with all concerned, that may not be the case," he notes. He believes that early communication is critical, especially when there are many vested interests represented.

Lessons

It is always good to get an early start on the communications effort. Likewise, it is better to provide too much information than to fail to keep constituents informed.

Advice

- Do not become discouraged by initial defeats, such as negative legislative hearings.

- Expect the unexpected from the many constituents with whom you work.

- When dealing with a major project, thank everyone who has supported you, even if the project is not successful.

Comments

In this case, the chancellor ultimately remembered the ninth shall-not. He drew in relevant faculty members by seeking their advice in planning for the new facility. He also remembered the first shall-not: He kept the community's trust by including opposing community members in the planning process. The way the chancellor handled this case is informative and instructive. The chancellor did not turn· to other presidents or chancellors for advice. Realizing that the major issue facing the college was ultimately a political issue, he sought advice from people familiar with the political process. He also used his own knowledge of the political process to achieve the college's goal.

THE NAME GAME

Many community colleges are relatively new members of the nation's system of higher education. But newness does not mean lack of identity. The choice of a name quickly establishes the identity of a college, especially if the name identifies the college with a specific place, such as a city or county. People associated with the region are proud of the name and may become defensive if anyone suggests changing it. Yet changes may be required to ensure that the college's name accurately reflects its mission or service region. For example, in the 1950s and 1960s many junior colleges changed their names to "community college" to bring their names in line with their mission. Other colleges outgrew their names as their service regions expanded, and they changed their names accordingly. To radically change the name of an existing college can be a major challenge for a president. Even when handled properly, such a change can create unforeseen problems for the college.

Circumstances

Located on the East Coast, Smyth County College had operated successfully for years as a junior college that emphasized the transfer function. As the college grew, it became more comprehensive in its program offerings and more accessible to an increasingly diverse group of students. Recognizing that the college's mission was changing, the governing board hired out-of-state consultants to review the college's mission. One of the recommendations made by the consultants was that the college change its name to include the words "community college," which would more accurately reflect its mission. Although the consultants did not recommend that "Smyth County" be dropped from the name, the president of the college pointed out that the college served five other counties and a city in addition to Smyth County. Now, he proclaimed, was the time not only to add "community college" to the name but also to change the name to indicate that the college served more than Smyth County. The president assured the governing board that the name change would not present a problem, for he had all along been referring to the college as a community college in the hundreds of speeches he had given during his six-year tenure as president.

Although the president did not anticipate any problems with the name change, he nevertheless carefully and systematically set out to cover all bases, for he recalled that a few years earlier a hospital in the area had encountered strong opposition when its board decided to change its name to reflect its geographic area. The president contacted members of the boards of supervisors and the city council in the jurisdictions served by the college to explain the proposed name change and to ask for their support. He spoke with all of them except one member of the city council who was unavailable to meet with him. As it happened, the elusive council member had a well-deserved reputation for being in the opposition most of the time.

The missing council member soon surfaced on talk radio. He made an emotional argument opposing the

The missing council member soon surfaced on talk radio.

name change, a stance supported by the talk-show host. In addition, the council member gave a negative view of the college in general. What had started out as a straightforward proposition—to change the name of the college to reflect more accurately its mission and geographic area—had become a public relations nightmare. In spite of his carefully laid plans for the name change, the president now faced a major problem.

Seeking Help

The president first turned to a member of the hospital authority from the hospital that had recently changed its name to reflect is regional nature. That person informed the president that the same city council member who was now opposing the change in the college's name had also opposed the change in the hospital's name and had never gotten over losing the battle to preserve the old name. The president of the college was now reaping the council member's anger, said the hospital authority member. He advised the president not to ignore the critics of the name change, but rather to respond to them. Having consulted someone whose agency had faced a similar problem, the president was now able to view his problem from a broader perspective and to profit from the lessons learned by the hospital authority.

Taking Action

The president decided to take a bold and risky step. He would take his case—the college's case—for a name change directly to the public. He appeared on two radio talk shows and presented his case. He found that there was strong public support for the name change. What opposition there was evaporated quickly. The ceremony officially changing the name of the college attracted members of the power structure of the community, including the mayor, county supervisors, and members of the city council, all of whom were supportive of the college's name change and its role in the community.

The president knew that although he had successfully swayed public opinion in support of the name change, the council member who had opposed the change remained a potential problem, for he had a small but vocal following in the community. The president's approach was "to be extremely courteous and solicitous of this gentleman as if he had been one of our strongest supporters." The approach worked: The council member attended the college graduation that spring, and later a member of his family graduated from the college.

Regrets

The president in this case feels that his only mistake was failure to persist until he contacted the council member, especially since the council member had a reputation for opposing change.

Lessons

Perhaps the most important lesson here is that there are no innocuous activities involving the college when one is dealing with an issue that affects the public—especially when local politicians become involved. That is, presidents should not take anything for granted; rather, they should plan carefully, as did the president in this case. The second lesson is that no matter how well one plans, things can and do go wrong.

Advice

- When faced with a problem, learn how others have handled a similar problem. Even if a problem appears to be unique, someone somewhere has faced and likely solved a similar problem.

- Avoid retaining enemies, if possible—especially those who have political influence in the community.

- Do all you can to win support for the college from all segments of the community.

- Be prepared to act on your convictions, even if that means taking chances.

Comments

It is almost always dangerous to take on a politician in public; to do so on talk radio was a bold move for this president, but it was the correct move. Not only did the radio appearances help solve the problem connected with the name change, they also gave the president a chance to say many other good things about the college. Indeed, what appeared to be a negative situation actually gave the president a public forum to promote the college. The president in this case remembered the third shall-not. If he had made the mistake of taking the politician's opposition personally, he could have made a personal enemy of his opponent by behaving in a superior or ungracious way after winning a public victory. This president wisely did not gloat but made sure to be extremely courteous to his opponent, which helped him win that person's approval later. Had the president acted out a personal emotional need to show that he was "right" in the public eye, he could have alienated the opposing politician and created the potential for future problems for the college.

WHEN VALUES COLLIDE

Circumstances

A southern college sponsored an exhibit of college photographs of gay and lesbian people at work. One was a nurse, one a firefighter, and another a kindergarten teacher. One striking photograph showed a politician speaking to a large group of college students. In the photograph, a banner hanging on the wall in back of the podium, just below the name of one of the state's leading universities, called for rights for gays and lesbians.

The college received several phone calls and letters protesting the exhibit. The controversy surrounding the exhibit was reported in the local newspaper. Especially incensed over the exhibit was the local member of the state legislature, who demanded an explanation of why the college was sponsoring "pornography." The trustees knew they would have to explain to the legislator that the exhibit was sponsored by a student organization and thus clearly came under the protection of academic freedom. They directed the president to draft a letter to the state legislator stating the board's position supporting the exhibit. The board chair was to sign the letter. The president was pleased with the board's stand and felt that the situation had been brought under control.

45

The exhibit was not only controversial but also ill timed, from the perspective of the chair of the college governing board. The chair was seeking election as a county commissioner and desperately needed the continued support of the state legislator who had written the letter protesting the exhibit; she certainly did not need a public confrontation with a member of the state's General Assembly. The county commissioner election was just eight days away. The board chair felt that the exhibit had already hurt her chances to win the election, and she knew that if the college board took a public stand in opposition to the state legislator, she would lose the race. Nevertheless, she came by the president's office the next day and signed the letter to the state legislator, as agreed to by the board.

The letter was lying on the secretary's desk waiting to be mailed when the president received a call from the board chair. The chair asked the president to hold the letter until after the election. The president did not commit himself. His own values called for him to mail the letter at once, but he wondered what difference it would make if the letter were delayed for a few days.

Seeking Help

The president called two of his presidential colleagues for advice. Both advised him to hold the letter until after the election. Members of the president's staff met to discuss what to do. Without exception, they felt that the president should not hold the letter.

Taking Action

The first thing the president did was "to weigh all the facts and consider all options available before coming to terms with my decision." The president did not call other members of the board, for he knew that at least two members would be happy to see the chair lose the election and would demand that the letter be mailed at once. He knew that the ensuing public debate would tear the board apart. The results would be damaging for the college. The president did not mail the letter until after the election.

Regrets

The mistake here, in the president's view, was not of his own making. Rather, it was a flaw in the college policy. The college had no procedures in place that permitted the president to call the board together or to call individual board members to deal with controversial issues. The board chair was the only one authorized to call special meetings of the board, and sunshine laws made contact with individual trustees to discuss college business questionable. Some months later the board established a policy that would permit the president to call the board together, should the need arise.

Lessons

This president learned that compromise is tempting when one is placed in a tight spot. He notes that "as soon as the crisis was over, I realized that I had compromised my own personal values and ethics." He also learned that issues "often are not black and white; there is much gray."

Advice

- Be prepared to remind trustees of their role and responsibilities.
- Find ways to encourage trustees to evaluate themselves and determine if any of their actions have the potential to hurt the college.
- Encourage the governing board to evaluate policies and procedures regularly to ensure that emergencies can be dealt with effectively.

Comments

The president in this case had to separate his personal values from what was right for the college in this situation. In doing so, he adhered to the third shall-not: He did not let his personal values take precedence over the college's best interest because, at least in this instance, the personal compromise could be managed.

6

Votes of No Confidence

Few things can destroy the confidence, damage the pride, and hurt the feelings of a president more than a vote of no confidence from the faculty. Yet faculty members do exercise the vote on occasion. At times, presidents deserve to be called up short by the faculty for their actions. In other situations, the vote of no confidence may have little to do with who the president is or what actions he or she takes. For example, a vote of no confidence in the president may result from the failure of the governing board and faculty union to agree on a contract.

The Chancellor and the President

Circumstances

The president in this case had served more than three years as the president of one of four colleges in a multicollege district. His tenure had been generally smooth. The chancellor, to whom the president reported, had no major complaints with his performance, although she did feel that the president should be more aggressive in promoting the college. For example, the college badly needed new facilities to accommodate increasing enrollments, yet the president had failed to cultivate relationships with people in the community who could assist the college in obtaining funds for buildings.

This relatively calm situation changed when the faculty began to question the president's leadership. Questions led to more questions, and finally members of the College Faculty Association registered a vote of no confidence in the president. The president now had a serious problem, and one that concerned the chancellor as well. Once the chancellor became involved, it was only a matter of time until the governing board would become involved as well.

Questions led to more questions, and finally members of the College Faculty Association registered a vote of no confidence in the president.

The events leading up to the vote of no confidence seemed routine enough. They concerned three faculty members who had been reassigned and who were displeased with their reassignments. The college was well known for its rodeo team. In fact, its team had competed for the state championship for the past four years. Three faculty members, two of whom had been members of the team while students at the college, were given release time from teaching in their disciplines to teach in the rodeo program. But budgets were tight, enrollments in the transfer program were increasing, and the college needed to strengthen its core courses, following the recommendation of the regional accrediting body. These concerns caused the administration to relieve the three faculty members from teaching in the rodeo program and to reassign them to full-time teaching in their disciplines. The faculty members let the president know of their displeasure. As a compromise, the president offered to let them teach courses in the rodeo program on an overload basis. They refused. Later they informed the president that they would be satisfied if he would agree to their previous teaching assignments. The president refused.

Two of the three faculty members began circulating memos among the faculty, claiming that the reassignment to their disciplines constituted a violation of their rights as faculty and indeed of their civil rights as members of a college community committed to shared governance. Soon the College Faculty Association was involved in the dispute.

Before the no-confidence vote, the College Faculty Association sent out a survey seeking information on how the faculty viewed the president. An outside consultant retained by the association questioned the validity of the survey, pointing out that it was biased against the president. The consultant's views did not deter the association; the survey went forward. The results: Over 79 percent of those surveyed indicated that they were not satisfied with the president's leadership. Two days later, the association polled its members, and 83 percent voted no confidence in the president's leadership. One of the reasons given in the association document for the vote of no confidence in the president was that he did not respect the faculty's role in shared governance. The chair of the association told a reporter later that "we just do not like the way things are done on campus. We want to be involved in the process." An English professor told the same reporter that many faculty members had not been satisfied with the president's performance for the past two years. The association's next step was to notify the college governing board of the no-confidence vote and to ask that the president be assigned to a new position. However, the association resolution stopped short of recommending that the president be fired.

The major local newspaper published an article on the no-confidence vote. The reporter interviewed the chancellor to get her views on the situation. The chancellor told the reporter that she wanted to meet with members of the association to try to determine what its members felt the president could do to improve his performance. "The president has a good record, and I do not want to drop him just because he has encountered some criticism," the chancellor told the reporter.

Seeking Help

The chancellor immediately sought the advice of other chancellors and presidents who had been through similar experiences. She notes that "the advice of your peers can be invaluable. But ultimately you are the one who knows your community best and the specific circumstances you face."

Taking Action

The chancellor, working under the direction of the college governing board, met with faculty, staff, administrators, and students to work out a plan for enhancing shared governance on campus. Consultants from the statewide faculty and trustee associations were made part of the process. Some progress was made under the new plan, but dissension persisted. Next, professional mediators attempted to bring people together, but they too were unable to satisfy all parties in the dispute.

Further Developments

The chancellor felt that things were moving along rather well and that, with the help of the new plan, the issues surrounding the president's leadership would soon die down. But several trustees became impatient: They wanted the issue put to rest at once. Four board members were facing reelection and did not want any controversy facing the college when it came time to vote on their reelection. The board gave the chancellor two options: either buy out the president's contract or reassign him to another position, as recommended by the College Faculty Association.

At first, the chancellor refused both options, since she felt that the president had done nothing to deserve either course of action. She told the board, "If the president goes, I go." Although she got the board members' attention, she did not sway them to her way of thinking. She believed that she was a good chancellor and the one needed by the system at this point in time. Taking a deep breath, she told the board she would reassign the president.

Regrets

The chancellor feels the first mistake she made was that she did not develop a strategy whereby the board could delay dealing with the issue until after the election. Perhaps, by extending the technical assistance and involvement of mediators through the election period, she could have given the trustees a grace period before they had to reach a decision. But she feels that this strategy might not have worked, for some board members believed their survival as trustees depended upon removing the president. Still, she notes that she probably had nothing to lose by slowing down the process.

The chancellor believes that the president made a mistake by not heeding her advice to develop strong relationships in the community. Strong community support would have made it more difficult for the College Faculty Association to bring pressure on the trustees to remove the president.

Lessons

The chancellor now knows that "even the best of presidents who contribute significantly to the college can be brought down by politics and personalities." In addition, she had an old lesson reinforced: If a president in the system is in trouble, the chancellor also has problems.

Advice

- Always remember that the presidency is a political position, no matter what the administrative organization of the college or the system may be.

- Be careful to develop strong relationships with both internal and external groups, including the press.

- Remember that timing is critical. Avoid conflicts that can reach the board or the public during board elections.

Comments

The president in this case was relieved of his duties because he failed to maintain a close relationship with faculty members. All too often, when problems force intervention by the chancellor of a system, the faculty, the governing board, or both are involved. Considering the number of presidents who report to a chancellor rather than to a governing board, this case has much to offer toward an understanding of the presidency.

WEATHERING THE STORM

Circumstances

The president in this case had been president of a small rural college for five years when her problems began in earnest. She knew from the first day she walked into the president's office that she was definitely a woman—and a single woman—in cowboy country. Her predecessor, a white male, was the founding president of the college and had served in the position for 19 years before retiring.

During the first three years of her tenure, things were relatively calm, although almost from the beginning a group of faculty had tried to intimidate her by feeding negative stories about her to the press and writing her threatening unsigned letters. Rumors circulated about her private life. Early in her fourth year, the situation reached the critical stage when the faculty issued a vote of no confidence in her leadership. Because of the extraordinary amount of local publicity surrounding the college and the high profile of the president, who was prominent in some national organizations, the no-confidence vote received national attention.

Charges continued to be brought against the president as audits were performed and investigations were conducted. Three years after the no-confidence vote, the president was still in office. The press backed off, and things were moving forward at the college. The president notes that "most hell raisers just got tired and gave up, although some are still working behind the scenes to discredit me."

Three years after the no-confidence vote, the president was still in office.

Seeking Help

During those troubled years the president first sought spiritual guidance, turning to her minister for help. She also became friends with a very influential business leader who, she says, "saved me emotionally, pointing out that the situation was political and not personal." A former president of a community college in a neighboring state came to the campus and offered advice, as did another former president from a southern state who read the articles about the no-confidence vote. The president enlisted the assistance of a political consultant who helped her to keep "a cool head." She also hired an attorney.

Taking Action

The first step the president took was to ask the governing board to employ a mediator to help settle the conflict that had developed between her and some of the faculty. She next invited a team of educational leaders to come to the campus to "find the facts," to listen, and to report their findings..The president then formed a collegewide committee to study the report and to make recommendations to her based upon its contents. She asked the board chair to call a meeting of the board and to poll its members regarding their confidence in her. The board gave her a vote of confidence.

Regrets

The president believes the biggest mistake she made was to become frightened. "I became scared and cried openly in front of my colleagues. Fortunately, I did not cry in front of local people." A second mistake, she believes, was to trust too many people.

Lessons

The president learned that she is tougher both physically and mentally than she had thought herself to be.

Advice

- Contact someone who "has been there."
- Stay calm, see your doctor for advice on coping with stress, get plenty of rest and exercise, watch a movie, get out of town on a pleasure trip, and seek solace in prayer or contemplation.

- Learn to forgive. This is very difficult, but necessary if you are to lead effectively.

- Recognize that the presidency is political. Indeed, some people see "president bashing" as a sport, regardless of who occupies the office.

Comments

This president adhered to the third shall-not. She managed to separate her emotional need to be admired by her colleagues from her professional need to seek advice from experts, including legal counsel. Had she become mired in her emotional needs, she might not have been willing to admit that she needed sound advice from other sources.

7

RACIAL TENSIONS

Of all of the issues faced by the nation's community college presidents, none is more sensitive and potentially more explosive than that of racial discrimination. Presidents of "the people's college" are rightly concerned lest they be viewed as favoring one racial or ethnic group over another. The following cases illustrate how race can become an issue and how community college presidents have dealt with the problems associated with racial tensions. Such problems have the potential of extending well beyond the campus.

WHEN A GRIEVANCE IS FILED

Circumstances

At this college, African Americans made up 22 percent of the college enrollment, yet only 6 percent of the students enrolled in the degree programs in health care were African Americans. One of these was an African American woman enrolled in the college's respiratory therapy program. The student, who had an excellent academic record and was on schedule to complete her degree on time, encountered what she considered to be an unfair situation: One instructor, she claimed, graded her unfairly on a practical examination.

The student first turned to the chair of the health occupation division for help but was not satisfied with the results. She then consulted the college's chief academic officer to resolve what was quickly becoming a major issue in her life. Again she was dissatisfied with the conversation. The chief academic officer informed her that if she was still dissatisfied, she could file a formal grievance with the vice president for student affairs. The student filed the formal grievance.

With the filing of the formal grievance, the president of the college found herself in the middle of the situation, for college procedures required that all formal grievances come to the president. In the grievance, the student demanded that she be permitted to retake the examination. She did not allege racial discrimination in her grievance, so the grievance was treated as an academic issue involving alleged unfairness in the grading practices of one faculty member. Following college procedures to the letter, the president appointed a grievance committee to hear the case. The committee recommended that the student be permitted to retake the examination under a different instructor; she did so and passed the examination.

Two days before the committee heard the grievance, the president had received a letter from the student stating that she wanted to appear before the next meeting of the college governing board. In contrast to the formal grievance, the letter was inflammatory, charging the college with practicing racial discrimination. The student claimed that the president condoned racial discrimination by allowing it to occur on campus. Copies of the letter were sent to members of the college governing board, the NAACP, the ACLU, the state secretary of education, the Office of Civil Rights, and members of the state legislature. What had at first appeared to be purely an academic issue now threatened to become a public relations nightmare that, if not handled correctly, could threaten the president's tenure and tarnish the college's image.

State law permitted members of the public to address the college board in a public meeting. The student was informed that she could address the board at its next meeting. Reporters from two newspapers and one television station were present.

In her presentation the student claimed that she had been mistreated at the college and that the program in which she was enrolled discriminated against minorities. As evidence, she pointed to the small number of minority students enrolled in degree programs in the health fields. She also stated that the college's grievance procedure was difficult to understand and structured in a way that discouraged the filing of grievances. Although the board was not required to respond to presentations made by members of the public, the board chair nevertheless suggested to the student that she make her charges in a formal grievance.

The student filed another formal grievance, the president appointed a new committee to hear it, and the grievance process was once again set in motion. The grievance committee concluded that the student had not experienced racial discrimination; it did, however, make several recommendations, which the president accepted. The student was notified of the findings of the committee and of the steps the president would take to prevent future misunderstandings about the college's commitment to fair and equitable treatment for all students.

In her presentation the student claimed that she had been mistreated at the college and that the program in which she was enrolled discriminated against minorities.

The president recognized that the two grievances had exposed some mistakes that she and the college had made. She also realized that the grievance procedure at the college was indeed difficult to follow, especially for a student who had to rely upon the assistance of busy and hard-to-reach, top-level administrators. Her immediate goal was to make sure that similar situations did not occur in the future.

Seeking Help

The only person the president consulted regularly in this case was the college attorney.

Taking Action

Although the president believes that the case demonstrated that the student had not been discriminated against on the basis of race, she still took several actions as a result of the case. She spoke with members of the local NAACP chapter and invited them to sit in on the second grievance hearing. One member accepted the invitation. The faculty member accused of racial discrimination was informed of his rights in the process and was assured that the college would see that his rights were protected. Although the student chose to make the issue public in an inflammatory way, the president never dismissed the student's concerns. The college investigated every allegation made by the student. The president kept members of the board informed at all times. The college's grievance procedure and all related procedures were reviewed and revised, and made available to all students. Information was gathered and analyzed regarding minority enrollment in "limited access" programs, such as degree programs in the health technologies. An ongoing program on cultural diversity, including diversity training for the faculty and staff, was put in place. Finally, media relations training was initiated, and a plan developed for use in any future public relations crisis.

Regrets

"I made many mistakes in this process, none of which was fatal," the president says. Her first mistake, she believes, was to assume that she had accurate and complete information on the initial grievance, when this was not the case. A second mistake lay in not examining the student's concerns more carefully. "I believe that if others in the process had been better listeners and responders, the matter could have been resolved before it became formalized and public," the president notes. Another mistake was that the president kept her distance from the student to be sure that she remained impartial. "In retrospect, I should have spoken with her immediately to be sure that I understood her concerns and the issues surrounding the case." Finally, the president mistakenly assumed that the college's grievance procedure was adequate. As the case progressed, "it became obvious that the grievance procedure was unsatisfactory for many reasons."

The president notes that this case was complicated by the allegation of racial discrimination and by the student making her case public. The president had to ensure that everyone involved was treated fairly. In addition, the process had to be managed carefully in order to prevent a public relations disaster.

Lessons

The president in this case learned the true value of good media relations. From the start of her tenure, she had been honest with representatives of the media. One result was that the television station did not air the grievance story. The two newspapers spent considerable time gathering facts concerning the student's claim of discrimination. One of the reporters sat in on the second grievance hearing, a permissible act because grievance hearings are open to the public in that state. As a result of the president's work with the media, two well-balanced stories on the racial discrimination grievance appeared in the local papers. The president also learned that one should never assume that a grievance is not valid simply because it does not follow established college procedures. (The student was late in filing the formal papers required in the grievance procedures.) A final lesson was that seemingly routine issues have the potential to cause major problems for a college.

The events associated with the grievance took their toll on the president, her spouse, the college board, and members of the college community. The student also devoted large amounts of time and energy to the grievance.

Advice

- Make sure that the "facts" in any situation are indeed facts, even if it means you have to gather them yourself.

- Develop procedures to ensure that students have easy access to the grievance process and that they receive all necessary assistance.

- Establish a process for reviewing policies and procedures routinely rather than waiting until a crisis occurs.

- Have a plan to deal with public relations emergencies.

- Work constantly to maintain positive relations with the media.

Comments

The president in this case handled the situation well. She did not become defensive, even in the face of the student's sometimes inflammatory actions, and she maintained a balanced perspective that allowed her to see ways to improve the grievance process. In doing so, she adhered conscientiously to the first shall-not: She never betrayed the public trust, and the trust she had fostered with media representatives and other constituents stood her in good stead. She also fulfilled her commitment to uphold students' trust by viewing the situation as an opportunity to revise and improve the grievance procedure.

THE INVITATION

Circumstances

The president of a southern college hosts a luncheon each year to commemorate Black History Month. Invited guests are leaders from the community who are minorities. The president uses the occasion of the luncheon to bring the guests up to date on the college's efforts to employ a more diversified faculty and staff. The luncheon has enjoyed success during the 10 years it has been held. This past year, however, the president was presented with an unexpected challenge as he prepared for the luncheon.

A minority staff member chided the president for not inviting all minority staff members to the luncheon. The president explained that the luncheon was primarily for members of the community and that it had grown so in numbers that it was difficult to accommodate the invited guests, let alone all minority members of the college community. Although some minority staff members were invited to the luncheon, they were selected for their expertise and skills, not just because they were minorities. This fact did not satisfy the staff member who insisted that he had been passed over while all other minorities received invitations. In a conversation with another member of the college community, the staff member accused the president of discrimination. He continued to feed the rumor mill until it appeared as if a minor problem was going to explode into a major issue.

Seeking Help

The president immediately contacted a well-respected and trusted minority staff member who advised him not to make a major issue of the staff member's actions.

Taking Action

The president quickly realized that he and the college had a potential problem that could result in irrevocable damage to the college if left unchecked. The staff member whom the president contacted for help informed the president that he would take care of the situation, and he did. He was able to reason with the upset staff member, and the issue was resolved quietly.

Regrets

The president underestimated the problems that can occur when even one faculty or staff member is disgruntled, especially if the individual moves the issue to a level that involves the entire college.

Lessons

The most important lesson this president learned was that one should think carefully about how an individual will react in a given situation and talk with the person in advance to ensure that he or she understands clearly what is happening and why things are done the way they are done. Every campus has its "lightning rod" in any given situation. Presidents should know who they are and make sure they have the facts in any case in which they might have an interest. The red flags are often there; presidents should not ignore them, even if talking with certain faculty or staff members is not the high point of their day.

Advice

- Do not ignore your critics, but be careful not to respond to them so vigorously that a nonissue becomes a major issue requiring vast amounts of presidential time and energy.

- Understand, develop, and use the informal network at the college. As was true in this case, a staff member in a support position gave the president better advice and suggested a better course of action than was available from anyone else on campus, including the vice presidents.

- Keep in mind that seemingly routine issues have the potential to cause major problems for the college.

Comments

This president benefited greatly from having established good trust and communication and a close working relationship with staff.

COMBINING POSITIONS

Circumstances

A president of a northwestern college that formed part of a statewide community college system made the decision to combine several academic departments and divisions into three divisions. Three deans were to be recruited to fill the newly created positions. The goal of consolidating the departments and divisions was to operate the college more efficiently, thereby saving money. The president, acting according to college procedures, appointed three search committees to assist in filling the vacancies. The committees had representatives from the existing divisions and departments that were to be absorbed into the new divisions. Current employees were invited to apply for the new positions.

Things went well with the first two searches. The third search, however, encountered some difficulties. The chair of one of the divisions that was to be absorbed applied for the third deanship. He was a minority male. Another division chair, who was white, also applied for the position, as did several other people. Four made the final cut: the minority administrator, one white woman, and two white men. The minority candidate campaigned hard for the position, contacting local political and community leaders. He also approached the chancellor of the system regarding the position.

Before a decision was made to offer the position to one of the candidates, the minority applicant lodged a complaint with the chancellor of the system claiming that some members of the search committee were biased against him because of his race. He asked that two members of the committee be replaced. The college president, the affirmative action officer, and the system chancellor discussed the issue and decided, on the recommendation of the president, to disband the committee in an attempt to ensure that no members be "branded as biased."

Upon hearing that the committee had been dissolved, the campus senate and other faculty and staff members quickly became involved, siding for the most part with the search committee. Those committee members accused of bias filed grievances to discover the content and basis of the charges. To complicate the situation further, members of the college community refused to serve on a new search committee should one be appointed.

Seeking Help

This president sought help from the academic vice president, an attorney, and his spouse, also an attorney.

Taking Action

The first action taken was to cool off the situation by discontinuing the search and appointing an interim dean. None of the applicants for the position was considered for the interim post. The president met with the affirmative action officer and the chancellor and explained how he felt the issue should be handled. He worked hard to ensure that all those involved, including the original search committee, were kept up to date on what was happening. He shared with the college community everything that permitted by law, a move that helped keep calm. He saw to it that the four applicants for the dean's position were all kept informed of what was taking place.

Regrets

"In hindsight, I didn't give enough thought to the composition of the search committee, even though I knew that the minority male's division had been very troubled and divided for some time," explains the president. He believes that he should have anticipated the actions of the minority applicant and thus been better prepared for what happened. Finally, this president failed to understand "how close to the surface racial tensions are on campus." He believes that the "bad feelings and racial tensions that have arisen from this episode will probably taint the campus environment for a long time." The president notes, "I worry that the accelerated pace of decision making and the overload of work may have caused me to rush into this one too quickly and without thought for the consequences of some of my choices."

Lessons

The president in this case learned just how sensitive racial issues are on campus. He also learned that "things that seem fairly simple, such as putting together a search committee, may need more attention than I gave in this situation."

Advice

- Take extreme caution with racial issues, for they are almost always emotional, threatening, and incendiary.
- Be sure to give accurate and copious information when such an issue arises.

Comments

This president paid careful attention to the second shall-not. He kept all parties informed who had a stake in this situation, including the other applicants for the position. As he himself notes, he could have been more aware that one applicant's division had been troubled and divided. This emphasizes the importance of the ninth shall-not.

8

OBSERVATIONS AND RECOMMENDATIONS

Although each of the situations discussed in the previous chapters is unique in its details, they share common themes. The following observations identify these themes, providing another perspective from which to view the difficult issues and problems faced by presidents. The observations are followed by several recommendations, largely based on the cases presented here.

Observations

Few, if any, of the cases discussed in this book were sensational in the sense that they would make the headlines in *The Chronicle of Higher Education*. Rather, most dealt with issues that are faced daily by presidents across the nation. By viewing these issues as daily occurrences, it becomes clear that the presidency is not about headlines—whether to make or avoid them—it is about working hard day in and day out, year in and year out. No problem is small or insignificant if the president's office must deal with it. This observation is especially true if someone else creates the problem and the president has to be brought in to solve it.

In most cases, the presidents involved in the cases recounted here took the high road and resisted the temptation to violate one or more of the presidential shall-nots. This observation speaks well of the ethical standards that presidents in this study set for themselves and adhered to during trying situations. From this, it seems safe to expect that the majority of community college presidents would hold themselves to similarly high standards if faced with similar situations.

Presidents want to perform well, and when they do not, they suffer from physical and mental stress. Several of the presidents responding to the survey reported they wept openly, meditated or prayed, had to resist the temptation to drink alcohol to excess, turned to physical exercise, and took other measures to maintain their mental and physical balance during difficult times. A cynic might suggest that the stress resulted from fear of losing their positions. That fear is always present when a president faces a difficult situation; nevertheless, for most presidents, I think the fear of being fired is far outweighed by the fear of being viewed as a failure. I am confident that the physical and mental stress recounted in these cases came from the fear that one might not be the best president one could possibly be.

Presidents and the leaders of the Presidents Academy have debated the need for a code of ethics for presidents. The cases discussed here illustrate that the 10 presidential shall-nots, though not intended as a formal code of ethics, provide good boundaries for most presidential decisions. Presidents should think of the shall-nots as a set of common-sense rules that all presidents who wish to be successful *must* play by. The cases in this study clearly show that playing by the rules is indeed the best policy.

There is a need for presidents to monitor college rules, regulations, and policies carefully and regularly. If necessary, they should consult an attorney. But if it takes an attorney to interpret college policy, then it is likely the policy should be rewritten. College policies, if up-to-date and followed to the letter, are often the president's best friend. Even the rare, dissident trustee may be cowed when the president points out that college policy is being violated. In several of the cases discussed here, the presidents used college policies to

their advantage. For example, one
president used the occasion of dealing
with a grievance as an opportunity to
revise college policy. Presidents

*College policies, if up-to-date and
followed to the letter, are often
the president's best friend.*

should insist that the faculty and board manuals be revised regularly, or else
they may lose an important weapon in many of the fights they encounter. If
a case reaches the courts, the president who has adhered to college policies is
likely to be in a strong position to win the case.

Chief executive officers in any type of organization need to understand
the importance of institutional culture. New presidents should take care to
become acquainted with the culture of their new institution before they set
out to make changes. Failure to identify the institutional culture and to
make sure one is operating within boundaries that members of the college
community are familiar with and live by often dooms the president, if not
to failure, then at least to unnecessary frustrations and delays.

The community college president should expect the unexpected. Faculty
and other members of the college community, trustees, and members of the
public may at any time make a major issue out of a seemingly innocuous situation. As the cases illustrate, the president occupies a political position and
is subject to the tugs of the political process from both inside and outside the
institution. Presidents must try to ensure that minor problems remain local
and are handled efficiently and effectively.

An observation that may come as a surprise to some faculty and other
members of the college community is that successful presidents must and
often do compromise. Presidents should view compromise as an acceptable
option, and not as a negative act or, worse, defeat. Compromise is what
makes diplomacy, business deals, the political process, and the community
college presidency work. The act of compromise may help a president keep
things in perspective, for no one is right all of the time. If a compromise in
a particular situation is good for the college, the president should compromise, even if it means that he or she will no longer be seen as invincible. And
as some of the cases illustrate, the decision not to take action may be a form
of compromise, especially when a president's style and inclination are to act
when faced with a problem.

Based upon the cases in this study, a surprising observation is that many presidents did not seek help through the informal network on their own campuses. In only one case did the president turn to someone outside the "official circle." The lack of references to informal networks in the survey responses may well be a result of the nature of the cases discussed. In any event, as the many presidents who do turn to their college's informal network can attest, faculty leaders and other members of the college community can give invaluable advice to a president, thus helping prevent or ward off many potential problems for both the president and the college. Presidents should identify and cultivate these networks and use them extensively.

Faculty leaders and other members of the college community can give invaluable advice to a president.

As quite a few presidents can attest, a vote of no confidence is not necessarily fatal to a presidency. Presidents in many cases have dealt with a vote of no confidence and survived. As the cases show, some have even used the vote as a catalyst for improving their performance. These presidents took actions that made the vote of no confidence less threatening than it appeared to be in the beginning.

Racial tensions may be near the surface on some campuses—a fact presidents should acknowledge. Every president, regardless of his or her race, gender, or ethnicity, must do all that he or she can to ensure that any perception of racial prejudice or discrimination is dealt with quickly and effectively. If the community college is to fulfill its role as one of the nation's premier democratic institutions, all signs of racial discrimination must be erased. Presidents must naturally take the lead in seeing that this happens.

Presidents should never burn their bridges when leaving a position, regardless of the circumstances under which they leave. From a personal perspective, those presidents who do burn their bridges are often bitter and cynical and never seem to get their lives back on track. From a professional perspective, when presidents are dismissed, they are likely to seek another community college presidency, or at least a high-level position. The circle in which presidents operate is a small one, and word of a particular president's behavior is sure to get around. Anytime former presidents seek a new position, they encounter the past. If the former president criticizes his or her former board, vice presidents, faculty, members of the community, and others, he or she is unlikely to be hired for the new position. Few colleges want to employ people who complain about their previous circumstances. In addition, presidents who burn their bridges make it very difficult for the people they list as references to speak positively about them. Presidents should remember that most presidencies are not lifelong positions; thus, they should prepare themselves for life after the presidency. One way to do this is to build and maintain strong relationships. To willfully destroy relationships is to lose a part of oneself and can result in professional isolation.

How long is too long for a president to remain in a given presidency? Certainly there is no canonical number of years. Many presidents remain effective for decades, others for only a short time. Yet there are some signs that a president should watch for, which may indicate that it is time to move on. One president, at the relatively young age of 57, decided to "step down" after over two decades in the presidency at one college. In making his decision, he took into account the usual reasons: The job became repetitive, in spite of his many accomplishments and the good salary, status, and perquisites associated with the position. This president found that it was often necessary to either fight or ignore the local power structure, most of whom preferred low taxes to quality education. One local leader who constantly attacked the college, and thus the president, was the editor of the local paper. This president simply became tired of the battles and wanted more time for family affairs. He did not want to become bitter, and time in the system provided financial security. Thus he could think about moving on. As this president notes: "One needs to get out before one is catapulted out." This president wisely observed that "there is no magic point. Each person has to make the call depending upon his or her own personal situation."

Another veteran president who decided to retire from the presidency suggests that "the best time to move on is when things are going well." This president recognized signs telling her that it might be time to move on. "I was finding that I was using the same 'Charge to the Graduates' year after year, even though times were changing. My regular meetings with legislators, county boards, and contributors became matter-of-fact—they knew why I was there and what I wanted before I arrived. I was expected to belong to the same organizations, boards, and committees and to attend the same functions, banquets, and meetings. I loved what I was doing, but it had become routine." Each president should examine his or her own situation and decide how long is too long. The most dangerous sign is when the president becomes apathetic, giving all decisions and activities equal weight. When this happens, the president should step down and seek new challenges.

There is a need for current presidents to serve as mentors to those who aspire to the presidency. I have argued elsewhere that current presidents, not trustees, determine who the next generation of presidents will be. That is, trustees choose presidents from a small pool of candidates who have the blessing of current presidents. With this in mind, presidents have an obligation to mentor future presidents and to share with them what the presidency is like in difficult situations, such as those discussed in these pages. It is especially important that current presidents mentor minority and women candidates, who are currently underrepresented in the presidential ranks.

Finally, in times of trouble, presidents need someone to turn to whom they trust and who can give them sound advice. This observation is so important that the last chapter of this book is devoted to discussing how the Presidents Academy can help ensure that presidents can always find someone who can help them when they face a difficult problem or issue.

Recommendations

Several of the following recommendations grew out of the issues, problems, and observations discussed in the preceding pages. Others are based upon information on the presidency gained from other sources, including personal experience.

1. **Never take the board for granted.** Unless the board chair is actually the problem, always seek the chair's advice *early* when facing a problem. Work with the board to make sure its members understand their role and that policies exist to define that role. If trustees cross the line between policy and administration, tell them so, citing college policy if possible. Remember that the board and president have to work as a team.

2. **Encourage trustees to work through the president's office** when dealing with members of the college on issues and problems that affect the college, and explain why they must do so.

3. **Draw upon your own experience when facing a difficult problem,** for you probably know more about how to approach it than you might think. Drawing upon personal experience can help prevent destructive panic. As president, you must appear self-confident, even if you really wish you could hide in your office.

4. **Do not take "it" personally, unless "it" really is personal.** Most issue and problems concern the office of the president and not the person who occupies the position. Occasionally, however, the president is the issue. When the problem *is* the president as a person rather than the office of the president, then the president and the board must carefully evaluate whether the president should remain in office.

5. **Understand that as president you must work with all segments of the college community,** the governing board, and members of the community.

6. **Understand and respect the college culture** while at the same time working carefully and cautiously to change the culture where changes are needed.

7. **Even in times of apparent calm, do not assume that things are going well.** Often a surface calm may overlie existing problems.

8. **Remember that a president's mental and physical well-being is necessary if he or she is to function at full capacity.** Do not turn to alcohol or drugs in time of trouble; stay physically fit; and do not become so involved with the presidency that you define yourself by the position. Have a hobby or some means of relaxing. Some presidents find prayer or other forms of meditation useful in combating stress; others travel to escape the pressures associated with the presidency.

9. **Expect the unexpected,** and have a plan ready for dealing with it.

10. **Be gracious when dealing with constituents,** including those whom you may personally dislike. Try not to keep internal or external enemies, especially those who have political influence.

11. **Make friends in the community who have influence and who can help the college achieve its mission.** If you have community support, you are likely to have the support of the college board as well. At the same time, do not neglect internal responsibilities. You might raise millions of dollars, sit on the Chamber of Commerce board, serve as president of the Rotary, and in general promote the college in the community in every way possible, yet you might still fail if you lose the support of the faculty and do not understand and support the teaching and learning activities of the college.

12. **Always deal with the media honestly.** The media are not, or at least should not be, the enemy. Good media relations can salvage a president's career in times of crisis.

13. **Understand and use college policies** in every case that involves a policy issue. If an issue demands a policy and no policy exists, see that one is developed. Remember that policies are designed to bring order, fairness, and efficiency to the operation of the college. Be sure to have and use a process for reviewing policies and procedures on a regular basis.

14. **When necessary, involve the college attorney in decisions that have legal implications.** If you should face a problem that is beyond the responsibilities of the college attorney, then you should be prepared to hire your own attorney. Never use the college attorney for personal legal advice.

15. **Cultivate and use an informal network at the college.** Internal members of the college community are an invaluable resource and one that is underused by many presidents.

16. **Respond to criticism,** but stop short of permitting dissident groups to create an issue where none exists. This advice is especially useful when a president must deal with such emotionally charged issues as racial discrimination, union negotiations, and faculty discontent.

17. **Know how far you are willing to compromise,** and under no circumstances cross that line. The 10 presidential shall-nots are a good starting point for establishing the boundaries that you will not cross, even at the risk of being fired.

18. **Use good judgment in deciding when and where to apply pressure** and when to back off. A president who comes on too strong may jeopardize the situation as much as one who is too relaxed.

19. **Do not wear out your welcome.** Decide how long to stay in a position, and if you feel it is time to go, then go.

20. **Do not burn your bridges,** for you will probably need to cross them again at some time in the future.

21. **Above all, find someone to turn to when things are not going well.** This should be someone whom you can trust, as well as someone who has experience and knowledge, and who can help you solve problems.

Enhancing Presidential Leadership in a New Century

The community college presidency offers excitement, challenges, and rewards that make life atop the presidential seesaw worth living. Still, as these cases vividly illustrate, the presidency can be very difficult and frustrating at times. One major theme that emerges from the cases is that in times of trouble, presidents need someone to turn to for advice, comfort, and reassurance. This person may be his or her spouse, a good friend, a partner, or a religious leader. Rarely, however, can these people offer potential solutions to the complex problems presidents face. What presidents need, want, and in many cases require if they are to solve problems and resolve issues successfully is advice and assistance from community college presidents who have faced situations similar to those the current presidents are facing. Only someone who has dealt with similar situations and had similar experiences can help the president maintain perspective and balance.

In some of the cases, presidents turned to their presidential colleagues and mentors for advice. Certainly this approach is helpful, but only up to a

What presidents need, want, and in many cases require if they are to solve problems and resolve issues successfully is advice and assistance from community college presidents who have faced situations similar to those the current presidents are facing.

point. For example, any one president has only a small number of close presidential colleagues and thus can draw on only a limited pool of expertise and experience. Presidents often have big egos or insecurities that may make it difficult, if not impossible, for them to disclose their problems to a close presidential colleague. Colleagues also have their own problems and agendas, and may not be able to offer advice or assistance when it is needed.

Is there a way to ensure that presidents will have someone to turn to in times of trouble who can offer sound advice based upon experience, knowledge, and success in solving difficult problems? I believe that there is such a way.

Lifelong Leadership

Only recently has our society treated its leaders as if life begins and ends with tenure in a single leadership position. In the early years of the Republic, Americans saw leadership as a lifelong undertaking. Streams of people continued to seek the counsel and advice of George Washington, Thomas Jefferson, and other leaders long after they had left the positions in which they had achieved success. What if Washington had retired after leading American troops to victory in the Revolution, or Jefferson after writing the Declaration of Independence, or Eisenhower after D-Day? These were vibrant, intelligent individuals who continued to serve their country long after they had "retired."

Today's society stands in sharp contrast to the past. Today, former presidents of the United States seem to concentrate mainly upon writing their memoirs, playing in celebrity golf tournaments, engaging in charitable work, or monitoring elections in other countries. They may return to the ranch, or seemingly disappear. In any case, they no longer play a major public role in shaping the policies of the nation to which they devoted the most important years of their professional lives. There are, of course, some exceptions, such as Jimmy Carter, but he has accomplished much of what he has done in his postpresidential years *in spite of* the system, not through it. Even their own political parties, with few exceptions, tend to politely ignore former presidents. The result is that the nation loses much of the knowledge, experience, and devotion that former presidents could bring to solving today's problems. The parallels between recent former presidents of the United States and retired community college presidents are striking and in many cases differ in degree rather than in kind.

Community college presidents, much like our nation's presidents, are for the most part ignored when they leave the presidency. They are often unwelcome on the campuses of the colleges they served for many years. (One has to be careful here, for as one of the cases in this book illustrates, former presidents who do not act professionally should not be asked to return to the campus.) Even if they are welcome visitors, however, former presidents often receive little more than ceremonial treatment and rarely are asked for their opinion on any matter of substance. One former community college president, when asked how he liked retirement, replied, "When the most exciting thing you have to look forward to is the weekly Rotary meeting, then you know life has lost much of its meaning." This particular retiree tried for several years to tap into some network that would use his two decades of experience as president. For the most part, he was unsuccessful, and thus joined other leaders who have been, if not rejected, certainly ignored by the system they love and helped create, and to which they gave much of their professional life.

Retiring Presidents: An Untapped Resource

Retiring community college presidents represent a pool of talent waiting to be tapped. Yet so far community colleges have failed to draw upon the experience and knowledge of former presidents in any systematic way or to any great extent. The result is a waste of talent that community colleges can ill afford. This talent should be harnessed and used. The essence of the following proposal is that those interested in the future and well-being of community colleges should view retiring presidents as a valuable resource and find ways to capitalize upon their energy, talents, expertise, and experience.

Today, many community college presidents who leave the presidency are far from ready to retire in the sense of wishing to disappear from public life. Most are healthy, vibrant, intelligent, talented leaders who want and need to make use of their skills and experience, but who for any number of reasons are ready to leave the presidency. The character of Captain Call in Larry McMurtry's novel *Lonesome Dove* found that "he was still the Captain, but no one had seemed to notice that there was no troop and no war." Unlike Call, newly retired presidents will discover quickly that they are not still the president. But like him, they will find that they no longer have a college to lead or issue to resolve.

The average age of community college presidents today is approximately 54. Nearly half of the current presidents plan to retire within the next six years—that is, at around age 60. Many of these future presidential retirees are not ready to hit the golf courses or fishing boats full time. Many would like to use their talents and knowledge to further the goals of the community college, without facing the daily pressures that accompany the presidency. Most do not know where to turn.

A New Kind of Leadership

What if the skills and experience of retiring presidents could be used on a regular basis? What if a pool of experienced, successful community college presidents could serve as a national example on how to use mature leadership? The result would be a new leadership strategy that would differ dramatically from current leadership trends and could serve as a model for the nation.

This new leadership strategy would differ from existing approaches to college leadership in an important way. Instead of drawing upon the experience of one or two people, presidents would be able to draw upon a pool of retired presidents with a wide range of experience. This would allow current presidents to seek an informed perspective on essentially any issue or problem that they might face. This pool of talent would be far greater than the knowledge of any one of its members, bringing many decades of experience to bear on whatever issue a given president might be facing. In contrast, most current community college presidents have been in their positions for only a few years and may not have any close presidential colleagues from whom to seek advice and assistance.

Those retiring presidents who would join the pool would have left much baggage behind on the doorstep of their last college and would enter the pool without a specific agenda for a particular college. Thus, no matter what the issue might be, the retired presidents could approach it without the burden of emotional involvement. They would be able to view the community college movement as a whole, rather than being tied to the assets, liabilities, priorities, and culture of a single institution. As illustrated in many of the cases, maintaining distance from a personal agenda—keeping one's perspective—has proven to be a valuable component of handling volatile situations.

The community college presidency is a relatively high-risk position. One result of this is that many presidents become conservative in their approach to leadership. They fear making a mistake that will result in embarrassment or even termination. As one president notes, many presidents do not provide the leadership they are capable of providing because they fear failure. Free of the fear of failure or embarrassment, those in the proposed leadership pool would be able to express themselves freely but not recklessly. It is possible and even likely that the pool of presidents would be able to think more deeply than was possible while they were in the presidency.

The community college presidency is, for the most part, a pragmatic office. In spite of the movement away from purely local concerns and toward more global issues, the presidency remains somewhat provincial. As leaders engrossed in day-to-day activities and concerns, presidents rarely have the time to reflect on the implications of their decisions for community college leadership, especially in the regional, national, and international arenas. Those in the pool of former presidents would have time to think, reflect, and perhaps even write for publication—a rarity for most active presidents.

Of course, most retired presidents could reflect, write, and think about issues without being part of an organization. Most, however, will feel unable to continue their professional activities without the support of a peer group, access to some network for exchanging ideas, and an arena in which to work. A group of retired presidents who remain interested in providing leadership to the nation could do much with time to think, interact with each other, publish their ideas, and assist current presidents. For example, every community college president, upon reflection, would like to go back to a given situation and "do it again," improving on the first attempt. The pool of retired presidents would have a chance to "do it again," this time with the benefit of hindsight and further experience.

The pool of retired presidents would have a chance to "do it again," this time with the benefit of hindsight and further experience.

These former presidents would be able to bring innovative and effective leadership to bear on the issues and problems faced by community college presidents. They could also become role models for retiring presidents of four-year colleges, as well as for retiring leaders in business and industry. Thus, they would not only help the nation's community colleges, but also serve as a national model.

Fulfilling Their Potential

How can the skills and experience of retiring presidents be used to promote the welfare of the community college and the nation? The following three steps are a beginning:

1. The AACC Presidents Academy, which has as part of its mission to assist current and future presidents to function effectively, should take the lead in forming an organization of retired presidents. The organization would consider issues facing the community college now and in the foreseeable future, with major emphasis on the leadership role of presidents. In addition to using their own knowledge to identify important issues, members of the organization could consider issues identified by the Presidents Academy, other segments of the AACC, the American Council on

Education, the American Association of Community College Trustees, and other national organizations.

2. The organization could serve as a clearinghouse for potential solutions to issues facing community college presidents. Current presidents should be able to tap into the pool of retired presidents and obtain information that would help them to solve problems and resolve a variety of issues. Members of the organization would publish material intended to assist current presidents in their jobs, building in part on the contents of this book.

3. Most important, retired presidents would be available to serve as consultants to current presidents, to governing boards, and to others who need their assistance. These presidential consultants should be grouped according to their field of expertise. For example, there might be groups specializing in program development, fiscal management, uses of technology, fundraising, conflict resolution, and board and faculty relations. Most current presidents could list other ways in which retiring presidents might assist them. The major problem is how best to organize the retiring presidents so as to make full use of their talents.

> *These presidential consultants should be grouped according to their field of expertise.*

Organizing Retiring Presidents

Membership in the organization of retired presidents should not be tantamount to joining the AARP or similar general-purpose organizations for retirees. That is, the organization should not be structured specifically as a support group for retiring presidents (although it could serve this purpose for some presidents). Rather, it should be an organization made up of people who want to extend and expand their professional careers and who want to share their skills and knowledge. Therefore, a requirement for membership should be a desire to extend one's professional career through assisting community colleges to operate effectively and efficiently—not as a president, but as a contributing member of a professional organization that draws upon one's experience as a president.

Only those presidents who have expertise in a specific area should hold membership in the organization, thus helping to ensure its professional legitimacy. Many presidents who have performed adequately or even outstandingly may never have become experts in any aspect of the presidency and therefore may be unprepared to offer assistance on specific issues. In reality, most presidents who have been effective in their positions could provide assistance to help other presidents resolve any number of issues. Nevertheless, the pool of retired presidents should be made up of experts, not generalists. Of course, the criteria would have to be determined and an application process established. Thus, if a current president needed help in a specific area, the organization would have one or more experts in that area, whether financial management, international education, conflict resolution, board relations, community relations, fundraising, the use of technology, or program development.

In considering this proposal, it is important to realize that some presidents truly want to retire in the more traditional sense. They want to play golf, fish, sit in the sun, travel, and do just about anything but be associated with the community college, especially the presidency. These presidents' wishes should be respected; they should not be asked to join the organization, no matter how much experience and expertise they might have. The purposes of the organization must be clearly stated and its membership carefully selected.

The proposed retiring presidents' organization would have to have a small staff of one or two people to provide support services, contacts, and other resources. Ideally, the AACC, through the Presidents Academy, should provide the home base for the organization.

The retiring presidents would also have to have a way to stay in touch with the issues facing community college presidents. As anyone who has left the presidency has discovered, it is difficult to stay current unless one can regularly tap into what is happening at the presidential level. The organization of former presidents would provide one avenue for staying in touch with issues facing the presidency. For example, consulting with a president on an issue or problem would quickly bring members of the organization face to face with current issues facing presidents.

Taking Action

How would one go about forming such an organization? The first step would be to find out how many presidents plan to retire in the next two to three years. The second step would be to find out whether those retiring presidents would be interested in forming an organization of retired presidents. The third step would be to determine if existing presidents would consult with the organization. Fourth, leaders of the Presidents Academy and the AACC should decide if they and their organizations should play a role in using the talents of retired presidents and, if so, what that role should be. Finally, everyone who has an interest in the American community college and the welfare of our nation should ask if our society can afford to continue to waste the talents and skills of so many former presidents. If the answer to this question is no, then it is time to develop a new kind of leadership strategy that capitalizes upon the experience of seasoned leaders and offers their active colleagues advice, support, and inspiration.

INDEX

L

leadership, 50–52; lifelong, 78–79
leadership strategy, new, 80–82
legislatures, working with, 38–41
lobbyists, college, 40
lying, 1–2

M

media involvement, 42–45, 51, 54, 58–59, 61, 74
mediation, 52, 55
misappropriation of funds, 3–4
mission of college, 34

N

NAACP, 58, 60
name of a college, changing the, 41–45
network, informal: setting up and seeking help through, 69, 75
no-confidence votes, 49–56

P

personal issues of president, 3, 55, 56, 73
"petty cash," 4
police academy, 37–39
policies and procedures, college, 74
political appointments, 5
politics, 37–47. *See also specific topics*
positions, combining, 64–66
presidency, as high-risk position, 81
presidential colleagues, advice from, 16, 18, 19, 78
presidential seesaw, v–vi
presidential shall-nots, 1–7
presidential term. *See* resignation
president(s): after leaving presidency, 70–71, 78–79. *See also* retiring presidents; appointment to, 10–11; burning their bridges, 70–71; former, 10–13; leaving office before end of term, 52, 70; previous experience as, 13–14; public's confidence in, 2; reasons for slipping into undesirable situations, 7; role, v; staying too long in the position of, 6–7; transition following arrival of new, 15–21; of United States, 78–79; use of office for personal gain, 3. *See also specific topics*
Presidents Academy of American Association of Community Colleges (AACC), ii, iii, 68, 72, 82, 84, 85
pressure, applying, 75
public, going to the, 42–45, 54, 58–59
public relations, 42–46, 51, 60, 61. *See also* media involvement

About the Author

George B. Vaughan is a professor of higher education and editor of the *Community College Review* in the Department of Adult and Community College Education at North Carolina State University. Before becoming a professor, Vaughan served as a community college president for 17 years. He is author or coauthor of a number of books and articles on the community college, including *The Community College Presidency at the Millennium* and *Community College Trustees: Leading on Behalf of Their Communities*. He received the 1996 National Leadership Award from the American Association of Community Colleges.